EDITOR: MARTIN

 **ELITE S**

# SOUTH AFRICAN
# SPECIAL FORCES

*Text by*
ROBERT PITTA AND JEFF FANNELL
*Colour plates by*
SIMON McCOUAIG

Published in 1993 by
Osprey Publishing Ltd
Michelin House, 81 Fulham Road, London SW3 6RB
© Copyright 1993 Osprey Publishing Ltd

ISBN 185532 295 1

Filmset in Great Britain by Tradespools Ltd., Frome,
Somerset
Printed through Bookbuilders Ltd., Hong Kong

## Artist's Note

Readers may care to note that the original paintings
from which the colour plates in this book were
prepared are available for private sale. All
reproduction copyright whatsoever is retained by the
publisher. All enquiries should be addressed to:

Simon McCouaig
4 Yeoman's Close
Stoke Bishop
Bristol BS9 1DH

The publishers regret that they can enter into no
correspondence upon this matter.

## Editor's Note

Readers may wish to study this title in conjunction
with MAA 242 *Modern African Wars 3 South-West
Africa*.

## Acknowledgements and Author's note:

This discussion of South African Special Forces could
not have been possible without the assistance of K.
Meiring and H. Patterson of the South African
National Museum of Military History; (Naval) Capt.
Stephen of the South African Defence Force Public
Relations Office; Captains Appel and Claudine of the
South African Police Public Relations Office;
Commandant Moody, S/Sgt. DeAndrade Mientjies,
and the tireless Mrs. Mostert of Paratus Magazine; W.
Steenkamp; C. Melson; R. Crites; H. R. Heitman; Sgt.
J. Rautenbach; Commandant M. Needling; M.
Kaplan; I. Hart; G. Neate; M. Sullivan; M. Smith; M.
Rogers; Blackie and the many Special Forces operators
who gave their valuable time, effort, and energy, and
who wish to remain anonymous.

There can be no doubt that the military forces of the
Republic of South Africa are the largest, best trained,
and best equipped of any country in sub-Saharan
Africa. This book is limited, however, to a description
of the history, organization, training, uniforms, and
equipment of the élite units of the South African
Defence Force (SADF) and the special anti-terrorist
units of the South African Police (SAP) Forces.

For a catalogue of all books published by Osprey Military
please write to:

**The Marketing Manager,
Consumer Catalogue Department,
Osprey Publishing Ltd,
Michelin House, 81 Fulham Road,
London SW3 6RB**

# SADF PARACHUTE BATTALIONS

The Parachute Battalions long enjoyed the image of the toughest, most highly respected, and efficient fighting units of the SADF. Only recently has this position been challenged by the formation of the Reconnaissance Regiments.

The only South Africans to be parachute trained during the Second World War were a group of 50 officers who volunteered for instruction with the British forces. In the late 1950s the South African General Staff desired that an airborne unit be established. In 1960, 15 SADF volunteers were sent to the United Kingdom for parachute training at RAF Abingdon; of the fifteen, 12 were trained as parachute instructors, two as parachute riggers, and one in parachute drop procedures. These men, under the command of Commandant W.P.Louw, returned to South Africa to form the first South African airborne unit: Commandant Louw's 2 Mobile Watch was reorganized into 1 Parachute Battalion on 1 April 1961. By the end of 1961 the first South African paratroopers were enrolled for training courses given at Tempe, Bloemfontein. The Parachute Battalion established strenuous standards of fitness and became the élite of the SADF, known by the nickname 'Parabats'.

In 1963 the battalion was reorganized into the independent Parachute Training Centre and the Parachute Battalion; by 1967 these were re-combined. Elements of 1 Parachute Battalion were the first South African Army elements to see combat since the Second World War during Operation 'Blouwildebeest' in 1966; this joint operation with the SAP, against insurgents in South-West Africa, involved a helicopter assault on a terrorist base in Owamboland. When compulsory National Service was initiated, for

*2 Para Battalion on parade, 1989, with the locally produced Jakkals jeep in the foreground. (Paratus Magazine)*

a period of one year, starting in 1968, a strain was placed on the cadre of 1 Parachute Battalion, who were unable to administer both full-time National Servicemen and part-time Citizen Force paratroopers. Highly trained paratroops, who had completed their year of National Service with 1 Parachute Battalion, were ordered to conventional infantry units, thus wasting their expensively acquired special skills. To preserve this core of parachute-qualified individuals a Citizen Force parachute battalion, 2 Para, was formed in July 1971, based at Tempe; all National Servicemen who had completed their year of full-time training with 1 Parachute Battalion were transferred to 2 Para, which was composed of five rifle companies based separately across South Africa.

## Active Service

By 1974 1 Parachute Battalion companies regularly deployed to the South West African/Angolan border area to combat growing SWAPO activity[1]. In June 1974, 1 Parachute Battalion carried out their first operational jump at Bwabwata and Congola in the Caprivi Strip as a mop-up

[1] See MAA 242, *Modern African Wars 3 South-West Africa.*

force against SWAPO insurgents. The battalion first saw major action in Operation 'Savannah' (October 1975 to April 1976); 2 Para was also mobilized during this operation, and participated in the final phases, providing cover for the withdrawal of South African forces from Angola. Shortly after this action the size of the airborne forces was increased by the addition of a second Citizen Force unit, 3 Parachute Battalion. Both 2 and 3 Para provided companies for duty in the Operational Area as quick-reaction forces while mounting counter-insurgency operations, bush patrols and ambushes, manning observation posts, and participating in cross-border operations.

It was the opinion of the General Staff that the Parachute Battalions, operating as infantry units, were not capable of providing a balanced, effective, conventional force; an all-arms organization with an airborne capability was desired. On 20 April 1978 the three battalions were reformed with added supporting elements to form 44 Parachute Brigade; Brigadier General M.J.du Plessis and Colonel J.D.Breytenbach were tasked with co-ordinating the establishment of the Brigade. While the brigade was reorganizing the situation in the Operational Area grew

*1 Para Battalion jump from Dakota aircraft. The Dakotas are still in active service in the South African Defence Force. (Paratus Magazine)*

*A member of 44 Para Brigade signalling from the top of an air-dropped Ferret armoured car during Exercise 'Iron Eagle', 1987. (Paratus Magazine)*

▲
*44 Para Brigade on the march, 1987. The ballistic helmet with nutria cover and fold-up brim is worn, with the Pattern 1983 ammunition vest. (Paratus Magazine)*

*Members of 44 Para Brigade prepare to emplane for a parachute drop during Exercise 'Iron Eagle', 1990. (Paratus Magazine)* ▶

tense. Both 2 and 3 Para were mobilized and supplemented by a rifle platoon and mortar and anti-tank elements from 1 Parachute Battalion. On 4 May 1978 this group of 320 paratroopers, commanded by Col. Breytenbach, carried out a dawn attack on a SWAPO base 200 kilometres inside Angola at Cassinga, code-named 'Moscow'. Thus Operation 'Reindeer' was launched, inflicting heavy casualties on SWAPO with only four SADF personnel killed. Colonel Breytenbach was slightly wounded when the battalion was forced to evacuate the area by helicopter under fire from Angolan armoured vehicles. The operation was deemed a success.

The newly formed 44 Para Brigade saw action at Cassinga during Operation Reindeer (May 1978) with elements of all three Battalions deployed by parachute.

Since their first deployment the Parabats' primary role has been taking part in external operations, but they have also been deployed on internal defensive duties, providing airmobile reaction forces in the Operational Area. The brigade was formalized and expanded in 1982. Additional staff officers were absorbed and a Brigade Headquarters established. Other developments included the upgrading of sub-units to 44 Anti-Aircraft Regiment, 44 Signal Unit, and 44 Maintenance Unit; additional sub-units were activ-

ated including 44 Anti-Tank Company, 44 Pathfinder Company, 44 Despatcher Platoon, and 44 Provost Platoon. During the period 1984–86 Brigade elements and 1 Para companies performed urban counter-insurgency operations in the black townships of the Western Cape, Eastern Cape, Witwatersrand, and Pretoria during a period of intense political unrest. By 1986 44 Brigade was committed to defensive duties along the Zimbabwe and Botswana borders. During this time 1 Para elements were continually being deployed to Angola and South-West Africa while the Citizen Force Para units were involved in internal unrest situations. 1 Para sometimes provided companies to support mechanized assault groups during operations in Angola, where the paratroopers were also often deployed by helicopter.

In the early 1980s 44 Para Brigade tested the develop-

ment of heavy parachute drop capabilities. The tests were initiated in 1982 by 1 Para with lightened Land-Rovers, nicknamed 'Fireflies' and fitted with anti-tank weapons. These vehicles were air-dropped using either the Platform Load Extraction Delivery System (PLEDS) or the Low Altitude Platform Extraction System (LAPES). Though Parabat weapons, equipment, and uniforms are standard SADF issue, the brigade evaluated several unique designs of air-droppable, jeep-like utility vehicles, and finally chose the 'Jakkals' as standard. The Jakkals jeep (and the distinctive paratrooper jump jacket, or *slangvel*) are unique to the Parabats.

The first large-scale 44 Para Bde. airborne operation occurred in 1987 when 3 Para conducted Exercise 'Iron Eagle I' in the North-West Transvaal near the Botswana border. In this operation 500 troops, with vehicles and heavy weapons, were air-dropped from four C-130 Hercules, 12 DC-3 (US C-47) Dakota, and four C-160 Transall cargo aircraft.

In 1988 44 Para Brigade developed a full-time Parachute Battalion Group, along the lines of the Rhodesian Fire Force concept, which was to be ready at all times for immediate deployment. Several companies from 1 Para were placed under operational command of the brigade; and a composite parachute battalion was formed from these companies and from brigade assets and named 14 Para Battalion Group (the 1 referred to 1 Para Battalion and the 4 to 44 Para Brigade). The Group was given a new mission of amphibious assault in place of the traditional airborne role. After conducting an amphibious exercise at Walvis Bay the Group deployed to northern South-West Africa. In 1989, 14 Para Battalion Group was called on to repulse the final infiltration by SWAPO insurgents into northern South-West Africa; the Group deployed and was in the field with all personnel and equipment within 14 hours, and thereafter spent two weeks hunting insurgents in the Kaokoveld mountain area. In 1989 both 14 Para Battalion Group and 44 Para were de-activated.

## Selection and Training

These are rigorous in order to ensure a high standard of combat efficiency. National Servicemen are screened by 1 Parachute Battalion cadre each year during the training cycle to find volunteers for parachute training. Those chosen must pass a physical examination prior to a selection board which also screens the applicant psychologically. Those who are accepted are transferred to 1 Para to begin a three-month training course. This phase is followed by six weeks of advanced individual training. Throughout the training course the level of physical fitness is accelerated, culminating in an intensive two-week course that includes

*Men of 44 Para Brigade free an Armscor Jakkals jeep from its landing packaging during Exercise 'Iron Eagle', 1990. Most of them wear cloth nutria covers on their helmets and the paratroop jump jacket, or slangvel. (Paratus Magazine)*

*FN MAG crew of 44 Para Brigade during a simulated attack on a terrorist base during Exercise 'Iron Eagle', 1990. (Paratus Magazine)*

# THE PATHFINDER COMPANY

seven hours of training a day. This intensive training includes 16-kilometre runs while carrying tar poles; 'dogs'—automobile tyres attached to the trainees by a long rope; or the dreaded 'marble', a hessian-covered slab of concrete that must be carried everywhere the trainees go. During training, sticks of 12 men are formed to establish group esprit among the trainees. By the time training with parachutes starts, fifty per cent of the trainees have dropped out.

Two weeks of hanger training include land-and-roll exercises that progress to harness training, aircraft entry and exit drills in aircraft mockups, gantry training, active landing drills, parachute and aircraft orientation, and post-jump drills. After ten days of hanger training the first jump is made from an aircraft at 2,000 feet. The trainees jump in pairs. Seven additional jumps are required, including two by night and four with equipment, before the treasured parachute wings are awarded. Less than 30 per cent of the initial applicants finish jump school and earn their wings. Though their claim to the 'top slot' in the SADF may now be under challenge by some younger élite units, there is no doubt that the Parabats' training, toughness, and esprit match those of any airborne unit in the world.

The 44 Parachute Brigade Pathfinder Company was formed in November 1980 by Col. Jan Breytenbach, and organized to function as an independent force capable of conducting clandestine, unconventional warfare missions in the border region of South-West Africa and Angola.

When Robert Mugabe became the Prime Minister of Zimbabwe in 1980 the army was reorganized, with the result that many of the outstanding former Rhodesian units were disbanded. Many Rhodesians and members of the foreign element in the Rhodesian Army emigrated to South Africa. The Pathfinder Company was made up of expatriates from various countries selected from among former members of the battle-proven Rhodesian Army. The SADF was receptive to these professional soldiers, and offered bonuses for enlistment; 500 Rand, and a bonus of 1,000 Rand upon completion of a one-year contract.

A Pathfinder selection and training programme was initiated, lasting four weeks. The first stage of one week was conducted in the barren Drakensberg Mountains of south-eastern South Africa. The goal was to force-march a predetermined distance in an allotted time, under physical and mental stress, with a heavy load, and regardless of

*Parabat landing at Iron Mountain (Thabazimbi) during Exercise 'Iron Eagle', 1990. (Paratus Magazine)*

Having passed this test, the potential Pathfinders graduated to the second phase of selection which was conducted on the border with Zimbabwe. Basic fitness and soldiering skills were relearned, including patrolling techniques, navigation, survival, tracking, intelligence-gathering, and raiding, ambush and anti-ambush techniques. A five-kilometre live-fire assault course, consisting of wire obstacles, a water crossing, bunkers, and a simulated SWAPO encampment lent realism to this phase. Techniques for the selection of drop and landing zones was also practised. Weapons training progressed from the South African 7.62mm R-1 and 5.56mm R-4 rifles to the Communist Bloc AKM rifles that were issued for use on external raids.

The final phase of selection involved an assessment of the candidates' abilities in the operational area; they were deployed on SADF operations against SWAPO in South-West Africa's Sector 10, and in southern Angola. If the men proved themselves they then became Pathfinders. Each member of a four-man team or stick would be trained as a specialist in one field; the other members of the stick would be cross-trained in all the skills needed during an operation, for flexibility.

The mission of the unit was to locate landing and drop zones for main bodies of troops and to establish observation posts along SWAPO infiltration routes. The information gathered would be passed to Section 10 headquarters, which would then deploy the 44 Parachute Brigade Fire Force, helicopter gunships, or 32 Battalion to intercept SWAPO. The Pathfinders supported 32 Battalion on numerous external operations, operating in Buffel armoured vehicles, light utility vehicles, or on foot.

By early 1981 a group of Pathfinders was organized as a mobile strike force to harass and interdict SWAPO logistic routes. The strike force, code-named Sabre Ops, used nine customized Toyota Land Cruisers, Land Rovers, and Mercedes Unimog light trucks. Of the three Land Cruisers, one mounted a 20mm aircraft cannon while the other two each mounted Browning .50 cal. machine guns. The three Land Rovers each mounted a single FN MAG machine gun for the commander and twin, rear-mounted FN MAGs. The Unimogs each mounted one FN MAG, with one additionally fitted with a 60mm mortar; they also carried all the fuel, ammunition, and rations for the unit. All vehicles mounted smoke dischargers, winches, and puncture-proof tires. Communication between the vehicles was by VHF radio; communication with the base at Murrayhill was maintained by HF sets.

Shortly after receiving the new vehicles the unit was deployed to the operational area. Tactics were perfected, using pairs of vehicles together as teams—one Land Cruiser with one Land Rover. The Pathfinders were soon

weather conditions. Various checkpoints were to be passed. All kit was carried including rifle, seven days' rations, survival and medical gear, and water; the kit totalled 35 kg (77 pounds), and initially each two men would carry a crate of ammunition between them totalling an additional 35 kilograms. (After three days the ammunition crates were withdrawn and marching proceeded.) The men received both continuous harassment and enticements to quit from the instructors. Those who completed the journey in the set time were allowed to continue.

deployed with 32 Battalion against a SWAPO base. Unfortunately, the element of surprise was lost and most of the SWAPO forces fled; a small cache of weapons was seized. Upon completion of the operation the unit was moved to a new camp at Ondangua airfield. Subsequently, a number of short three- or four-day operations and a number of fighting patrols produced some contact with SWAPO; the Pathfinders achieved some successes, and took some casualties. In August 1981 the Pathfinder Company took part in the largest cross-border raid up to that time, Operation 'Protea'. Much valuable Soviet Bloc equipment was captured or destroyed, and hundreds of SWAPO insurgents and Cuban troops were either killed or captured; one Soviet advisor was among the captured and several others were killed in the fighting.

*Men of 44 Para Brigade prepare to board a C-160 prior to a parachute jump and simulated attack on a terrorist camp during Exercise 'Iron Eagle', 1990. (Paratus Magazine)*

One distinctive trait of the unit members involved their bawdy off-duty activities: a riotous sense of humour and various adolescent antics caused chagrin to the rather stiff South Africans. One favourite was the '44 Twitch': when driving in convoy and approaching another SADF unit the Pathfinders would all start twitching their heads and acting shell-shocked. Another was the singing of derogatory songs at mess when the unappreciated mealie-pap (a local staple made from corn meal) was served. Their SADF commanders overlooked these and other antics for the sake of the unit's value in the field. The company were

*Two Parabat Jakkals jeeps. The vehicle on the left mounts twin .50 calibre machine guns, that on the right a single FN MAG. The troopie on the far left wears a slangvel while all others wear nutria battle dress. (South African Defence Force)*

# THE HUNTER GROUP

nicknamed the 'Philistines' because of their uncultured behaviour, and this sobriquet was embraced by the Pathfinders as a badge of honour.

The South African government became sensitive to charges of employing foreign mercenaries, however; this was coupled with a lack of understanding for the Pathfinders' wild behaviour when not in the field, and when Col. Breytenbach transferred out of 44 Para Bde. the unit was turned into a training outfit. After completion of their contracts some members of the Pathfinder Company left the SADF, while the majority transferred to 32 Battalion. The company was disbanded in January 1982. The unit never consisted of more than 30 members, but wreaked havoc on SWAPO and its allies. Given the intensity of Pathfinder activity in the operational area the fact that only one member was killed in action was a true measure of the competence and professionalism of 'The Philistines'.

The Hunter Group, though little known outside the South African defence community, was the first counter-insurgency unit formed by the SADF in May 1968.

Commandant G.van Kerckhoven of the South African Irish Regiment, located at the Doornkop Military Base in Johannesburg, envisioned the transformation of elements of his regiment into a specialized, expertly trained counter-insurgency unit. Providing training that was consistent and superior to that given to National Servicemen was van Kerckhoven's goal. With the assistance of Mr. Grant-Grierson, a former member of the Rhodesian Forces and a weapons and unarmed combat expert, formal plans were developed for the creation of this novel and locally unique counter-insurgency unit, formed in May 1968 and named the Hunter Group. The scorpion was chosen as the unit emblem: Cdt. van Kerckhoven once said that 'the danger from the scorpion lies in the sting at the tip of its tail, not in the big pincers near its head where it is expected. Hunters

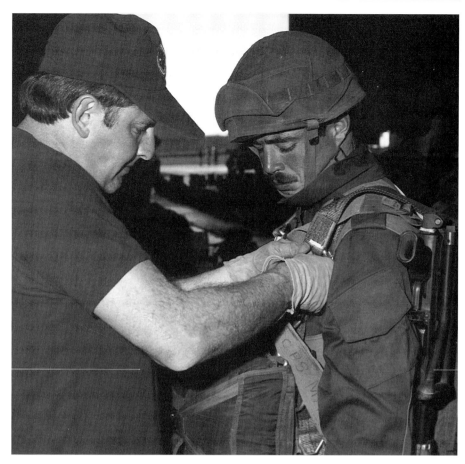

*A 44 Para Brigade dispatcher performing last minute checks before a jump. Note the dispatcher badge sewn to his cap, and the second pattern jump jacket worn by the para on the right—the second pattern has a flap over the sleeve pencil pocket. (South African Defence Force)*

*A lance corporal of 44 Para Brigade. Note the use of the para helmet without the nutria cover, the subdued embroidered shoulder flashes, and the khaki Denison-type smock. (South African Defence Force)*

operate the same way—our attack is never expected.'

The plans developed by Cdt. van Kerckhoven and Mr. Grant-Grierson were quickly put into effect, initial Hunter Group formation and selection procedures were established, and a cadre was formed from members of the Irish Regiment. Word of the Group's specialized counter-insurgency training and activities spread to other units in the SADF, and numerous volunteers arrived in Johannesburg to take part in training. The cadre provided training and administrative functions for the new arrivals. Trainees, who received no extra pay or allowances, participated in 240 hours of training over a twelve-month period at the Doornkop Military Base; the volunteer training was conducted at weekends and by night during the week. An added incentive for participation, however, was that the extensive training counted toward promotion.

Hunter Group training included unorthodox methods of tactics and patrolling, close combat training, parachute training, first aid, survival skills and bushcraft, vehicle driving, navigation, stress and shock training, working with tracker dogs, working with informers and the local population, aspects of guerilla warfare, riot control, mines and demolitions, and extensive weapons drill with the R1

7.62mm rifle. The weapons drill included a novel system of quickly positioning the weapon in order to fire instinctively at any target, from any position, similar to the 'Quick Kill' system used by the US Army a few years later in the Vietnam War and eventually adopted by the South African Defence Force; this drill trained men to unsling their rifles, turn, fall to the ground, find the target, and fire within two seconds. Hunter Group members rated as among the best rifle handlers in South Africa at that time. The members were also taught terrorist tactics and theory from experts who had seen fighting in Rhodesia, Angola or the Congo.

A special pattern of camouflage uniform was adopted: privately purchased 'splotch' pattern camouflage uniforms in a base colour of tan or green with various large splotches of green, dark brown, and black or mustard. Some of these uniforms were cut in an 'airborne style' of loose fitting smocks with both internal and external pockets and reinforced, padded elbows and knees. These uniforms immediately identified the wearer as a member of the Hunter Group, since no other SADF unit wore camouflage uni-

*Men of 44 Para Brigade exit a C-130 Hercules over the northern Transvaal* *during Exercise 'Iron Eagle', 1991. (South African Defence Force)*

forms at that time. A silver-coloured scorpion badge with an infantry green background was worn on the right sleeve by the volunteer instructor cadre who had completed 240 hours of voluntary training. Hunters who completed 42 hours of training wore a red scorpion on a saffron background on their left sleeve. A specially designed Hunter Group parachute qualification badge, and numbered identification discs, nicknamed 'luggage tags', unintentionally added to the unit's special mystique.

The Hunter Group graduates formed a core of specially prepared trainers and leaders in the Citizen Force. Over 700 men rotated through Hunter Group training; and many members later assisted in the formation and/or training of other specialized SADF units including 32 Battalion and the Reconnaissance Regiments. In 1976 the Hunter Group was reorganized into the Reconnaissance Commando (Reserve) and the 2nd Airborne Reconnaissance Company. Both groups were employed in an operational role along the South-West Africa/Angola border.

The Hunter Group, initially an experiment in counter-insurgency warfare, proved the feasibility, need, worth, and success of the counter-insurgency concept as taught to men drawn from standard infantry units.

# SADF 32 BATTALION

The SADF 32 Battalion was one of the most secret and controversial units in the South African forces. The unit saw more action along the Angolan and Namibian borders than any other in the SADF.

The creation of 32 Battalion was a direct result of the end of the vicious and bloody Angolan Civil War. A left-wing military coup in Portugal precipitated the Portuguese withdrawal from her Angolan colony on 11 November 1975. Three major groups attempted to fill the vacuum left by the Portuguese. The National Front for the Liberation of Angola (FNLA), the Union for the Total Independence of Angola (UNITA), and the Popular Movement for the Liberation of Angola (MPLA) all vied for control of the country. Since Angola holds vast deposits of uranium, titanium, gold, diamonds, iron, and oil, and a strategic geographical location in Southern Africa, it was inevitable that the superpowers would get involved. With United States backing, Holden Roberto's FNLA North and Daniel Chipenda's FNLA South formed an uneasy alliance with Jonas Savimbi's UNITA against the Soviet- and Cuban-supported MPLA and its military wing FAPLA (Popular Armed Forces for the Liberation of Angola), headed by Agosteno Neto. Other players in this game included China, North Korea, and Zaire, who supplied arms to the FNLA; the South Africans, who supplied arms to both the FNLA and UNITA; and the Portuguese Security Police (the DGS), who supported UNITA. With the superpower stakes escalating and the United States still traumatized by the Vietnam experience, US support to the FNLA and UNITA forces was officially stopped in December 1975. An increase in aid to the MPLA, in the form of massive Soviet airlifts of supplies and heavy equipment and thousands of Soviet-led Cuban combat troops, enabled FAPLA to achieve a provisional victory over the FNLA and UNITA forces in late 1976.

## Bravo Group

Specific troops from Daniel Chipenda's FNLA South group were trained by Col. Jan Breytenbach, the founding commander of 1 Reconnaissance Regiment, and his team of Recce Commandos at the start of Operation 'Savannah' in August 1975 at Mpupa, Angola, 70 kilometres north of the South-West Africa border. These troops were taught a style of guerilla warfare and tactics modelled on those used by the US Special Forces to teach indigenous troops during the Vietnam War. Cast-off South African equipment and battlefield pick-ups of Communist bloc weaponry,

*Refresher training prior to Exercise 'Iron Eagle', 1991. The instructor's jump boots and 'Tupperware' shoulder flashes can clearly be seen. After completing two years' National Service (reduced to one year in 1991) with 1 Para Battalion, troops are transferred to the Citizen Force unit 44 Para Brigade, where they are required to attend camps once a year. (South African Defence Force)*

uniforms, and field gear were pressed into use by the group. The use of Communist equipment was not only expedient, but also enabled the unit to live off and blend in with the enemy as an effective guerilla force. The group was organized into two rifle companies, a machine gun platoon, a mortar platoon and an anti-tank section. The FNLA force was given the title of Bravo Group, and was teamed with South West African Territorial Force 201 Battalion (recruited from Bushmen), or Alpha Group, to form Zulu Force. Zulu Force was put on the attack at the start of Operation 'Savannah'.

At the end of the war Bravo Group, now bereft of a homeland and leadership and with no certain future, might have become a possible source of trouble to the region. The South African influence over these troops was at issue since the SADF was pulling out of southern Angola as Operation 'Savannah' wound down. The South African Defence Force realized the value of this effective, battle-proven force, however, and ordered Col. Breytenbach to return to southern Angola to assemble these South African trained

*Troops attend the 44 Para Brigade selection course in 1981. Of interest is the Pattern 70 web equipment strapped over the Para-Fox rucksack, and the camouflaged folding-stock FN FALs. (I. Hart)*

ex-FNLA men and any other volunteers. These men were highly motivated and effective bush fighters, who knew the terrain of southern Angola well; they also spoke Portuguese, the common language of Angola. Some joined the South Africans for purely economic reasons, others joined out of hatred for the MPLA, which now sided with SWAPO. Col. Breytenbach set out to create a South African 'foreign legion' where loyalty was to the unit, or home, and not to any country; he saw this as one way to consolidate the members of the group, who came from seven different tribes. It was understood that once given a new home, the unit members would have to fight until age, illness, or wounds ended their useful service.

Once assembled, the headquarters was moved near Rundu, South-West Africa, close to the Angolan border. The troops were based at Nkurukuru, Dodge City (near Doppies), and Buffalo. Accommodation was spartan, with tents the only source of shelter for the officers, NCOs and single ex-FNLA men; the married FNLA men lived in barracks with their families. The group was commanded by white SADF officers and NCOs who signed up for one-year contracts consisting of eleven months in the bush with

one month's leave. It was difficult for Col. Breytenbach to convince the SADF of the validity of the concept of black regular soldiers officered by white SADF personnel, since there was only one black unit in the army at that time; so he proposed a politically attractive idea to the leadership—that since the unit would be used as a 'foreign legion', casualties would have no personal effect on South African voters. The SADF, always sensitive to the effect of battlefield casualties on South African public opinion, accepted this. (It should be noted, however, that the battalion's white officers have the highest casualty rate in the SADF due to the unit's established pattern of field leadership from the front. It also takes a special kind of white officer, given the background of the apartheid doctrine, to fit into this racially mixed unit.)

## 32 Battalion

The group was retrained, eventually re-equipped, and organized into a battalion. The unit existed somewhat independently, with little contact with the rest of the SADF. SADF equipment and weapons were procured, sometimes illegally, for their use. An operational base was set up 230 kilometres from the Rundu Headquarters. At this time the SADF changed the unit designation to 32 Battalion, to counter charges made by the Angolans of Bravo Group employing FNLA mercenaries. An aura of mystery surrounded these Portuguese-speaking troops, enriched by the secrecy of the unit and stories of their battlefield victories. According to numerous erroneous press reports the battalion were named 'The Terrible Ones' by their enemies. What is true is that the unit excelled at clandestine cross-border operations into Angola, earning the hatred and respect of their enemies.

The 32 Battalion counter-insurgency operations were mounted against the People's Liberation Army of Namibia (PLAN), the military wing of the South-West Africa People's Organization (SWAPO), and the FAPLA units which supported SWAPO and PLAN in their campaign to drive the South Africans out of South-West Africa (Namibia). The scenario for a typical 32 Battalion patrol against PLAN and FAPLA could consist of insertion into southern Angola by either foot or helicopter. In the early days a temporary base would be established from which reconnaissance patrols would fan out. In shifts, half the personnel would rest at the base while the other half patrolled for two or three days gathering intelligence. This patrolling could last up to six weeks. The temporary base would be moved to enable the area of operations to be completely covered. It was soon learned that companies as a whole had to move constantly and dig in at night to avoid ambush. The only SADF support would be helicopter supply sorties and casualty evacuation, and an occasional supply drop from C-47 Dakotas.

The patrols followed tracks, or spoor, through the bush. Enemy personnel would frequently be encountered in the evening while converging on water holes to replenish supplies. The contacts were usually fast, confusing, and bloody. Following the contact the 32 Battalion trackers would hunt and either capture or otherwise eliminate the escaping PLAN or FAPLA troops.

The battalion wear their own distinct pattern of camouflage uniform similar to the standard Portuguese pattern. A field jacket, shirt, trousers, and distinctive 'swallow-tail' or 'Bigeard'-type cap are available in three colour variants: a dark background pattern, officially designated Pattern 1, favoured by the Recce Wing; and a predominant brown for winter and a predominant green for summer, officially designated Pattern 2. All clothing items were 'sterile', untraceable to any specific country. Footwear usually consisted of standard issue boots. Since men of the rifle companies were issued with captured communist weapons, green nylon chest webbing to hold AK-47 magazines was issued. The use of camouflage uniforms resembling the Portuguese Angolan issue and captured Chinese- or Russian-made AK-47 assault rifles and RPK and RPD light machine guns gave them an appearance similar to that of FAPLA troops—and thus an edge in many contacts with the enemy. However, this resemblance to the enemy could also lead to cases of mistaken identity when encountering other SADF units, with disastrous consequences. Consequently, when used in the infantry role on operations with other SADF units 32 Battalion wore standard SADF issue nutria battle uniforms.

In early 1981 some of the secrecy surrounding the unit was lifted. A British former 32 Battalion lance-corporal offered his story to the world press. Allegations were made that 32 Battalion was led by white mercenary officers and NCOs across the Angolan border in counter-guerilla op-

*A rare photograph of three members of the Hunter Group in the field. All carry FN FALs, and wear the distinctive Hunter Group splotch pattern camouflage uniforms. (Anonymous ex-operator)*

erations; and that atrocities were committed against southern Angolan civilians. Though white foreign troops were part of 32 Battalion, only South African personnel led the groups. Since the unit operated behind the lines it had to rely on local inhabitants for information about the enemy and terrain, and to alienate them by committing atrocities would be a self-defeating tactic. At this time the South African government, sensitive to world opinion, acknowledged the existence of the then-secret unit. A reorganization of the foreign white elements took place in response to these charges: such men then serving in the

unit were asked to apply for South African citizenship or leave the service. A direct result of the allegations against 32 Battalion was that the SADF will now only accept South African citizens into its ranks.

Most NCO posts are now filled from within the battalion, except for certain senior or specialist NCOs. All NCO candidates are volunteers and are carefully selected from SADF infantry school graduates. The candidate must pass a rigid orientation and selection phase before being accepted into the unit. The orientation phase usually lasts one week. The NCO candidates are brought to a training area near Buffalo Base and outfitted with normal kit and equipment, two mortar rounds, and a small amount of rations; they are then divided into groups, briefed on the requirements and procedures to be followed, outfitted with a medical kit, and ordered into the bush by the instructors. Five days of constant physical training, exercises, marching, sleep deprivation, drills, and any other 'tortures' the instructors may demand are heaped upon the candidates. Those who survive the physical and mental pressures of the selection process are accepted into the battalion. Other courses are then required, such as advanced counter-insurgency training, and Portuguese language instruction, since all orders are delivered in Portuguese. The new junior leaders could look forward to six-week patrols in the bush far behind enemy lines, outnumbered by the opposition.

By 1983 the unit consisted of a reconnaissance wing, a mortar platoon, and seven rifle companies—A to G. The commander at that time, Col. Eddie Viljoen, moved the tactical headquarters from Ngiva to Ionde, South-West Africa, the new base being known as Fort Boela; this was a secure logistical base from which operations north into Angola could be supported. Battalion members lived on the base, forming a tight-knit community. Operations into Angola could last for as long as six weeks, with white officers and NCOs expected to spend up to six months in the operational area.

A 32 Battalion rifle company command structure consisted of a white CO, a white NCO as second-in-command, four junior NCOs and a black sergeant. Each junior NCO would lead a section of 14 African troops.

In 1984 FAPLA and Cuban forces were using conventional tactics against Savimbi's UNITA forces; the SADF would have to meet Cuban armour spearheading massive conventional FAPLA offensives. To effectively counter these forces 32 Battalion was retrained and restructured

*Presenting the 32 Battalion Colours during a public display, 1985. The battalion wear camouflage uniforms only when in the field, but retain their distinctive camouflage berets for public displays. (Paratus Magazine)*

*32 Battalion Colour Parade showing the distinctive company banners, 1986.* (Paratus *Magazine*)

with the addition of an anti-tank company consisting of a Ratel armoured car squadron, a battery of Valkyrie 127mm multiple rocket launchers, a battery of M-5 120mm mortars, and 20mm anti-aircraft guns. Support company was up-gunned with the addition of 106mm recoilless rifles, Milan anti-tank missiles, extra 81mm mortars, and Browning .50 calibre machine guns. By 1986 the battalion had been officially transformed from a guerilla and counter-guerilla force to a mechanized infantry unit with more firepower than any other comparably sized SADF infantry unit.

In 1985 the battalion was officially presented with its Unit Colour by the Chief of the South African Army. This was the first time that a SADF unit had received its colour in an operational area.

With the implementation of UN Resolution 435 in 1989, and the subsequent UN-monitored 'free and fair elections' in South-West Africa, the Angolan border war came to an end. The battalion was confined to its base during the peace accords between Angola and the Republic of South Africa; and subsequently became the South African military representative of a UN-sponsored joint military commission responsible for the control of the withdrawal of all South African forces from southern Angola, their replacement by the FAPLA, and restrictions on PLAN unit movements.

Thereafter 32 Battalion was pulled out of South-West Africa, now officially Namibia, and relocated to the old mining community of Pomfret on the edge of the Kalahari Desert in northern Cape Province 50 kilometres from the Botswana border. In 1990 the battalion was again called upon, being sent to Natal Province to quell tribal rivalries. The reputation of the unit remains high, and its fighting record is undoubtedly among the best of all South African units since the Second World War.

## 32 Battalion Reconnaissance Wing

32 Battalion organized its own Reconnaissance unit in 1978, instead of relying on the established SADF Reconnaissance Regiments. With Portuguese as the major command language, and the fact that the unit was a close-knit organization where officers had to prove themselves and lead from the front, it was more expedient for the unit to have its own Recce group. The 32 Battalion Recce Wing initially consisted of 12 men; by 1982 the number had risen to forty. In late 1983 the unit was disbanded and reformed at Buffalo Base with only one of the original members remaining. The Recce Wing eventually consisted of between 60 and 70 men based at Omauni, South-West Africa, about 500 kilometres from Buffalo Base; a high proportion of black NCOs were assigned to it.

The selection of Recce Wing members was not based on standard SADF requirements but rested entirely with the unit members. A group of officers and NCOs, known as the 'inner circle', consulted each Recce Wing member as to each recruit's performance in training. The new recruits were not fully accepted into the unit until having been proven on operations.

The Recce Wing operated independently of the battalion and frequently mounted clandestine patrols up to 250 kilometres inside Angola gathering intelligence against SWAPO and FAPLA. The rifle and mortar companies would subsequently act on the intelligence amassed by the Recce Wing. The specific mission was to conduct strategic and tactical reconnaissance, to use stand-off attacks to determine reaction time of the enemy, to study terrain, and to modify the existing out-of-date Portuguese maps of the

*The distinctive 32 Battalion buffalo head cravat, stable belt, and beret flash, 1985. The berets are made from SAP second pattern camouflage material. (Paratus Magazine)*

operational area. During 1981 to 1983 the SADF Reconnaissance Regiments trained with the 32 Battalion Recce Wing to gain bush experience.

When the Recce Wing was included in major operations its mission changed; it would then establish helicopter refuelling and administrative areas in the bush, and provide guides for SADF conventional units into southern Angola. This mission was later expanded to include ambushes, the initiation of a hearts-and-minds campaign, the development of the local populace into an intelligence network, and the harassment of SWAPO's logistical and infiltration lines.

The typical Recce Wing element consisted of a three- to five-man team, though larger groups could also be assembled. This team was known as a 'call sign'; a four-man call sign team consisted of a leader, a radio operator, and two machine gunners. The leader was either an officer or an NCO, known as the 'boss'. The boss navigated and led the team; his typical load consisted of a ground-to-air radio, a small pair of binoculars, night vision goggles, an AK-47 and 12 spare magazines, and 50 rounds of belted ammunition for the team's RPD light machine gun. The second in the team was the radio operator, who carried an AK-47 with seven spare magazines, a US M-79 Grenade

Launcher with 20 HE rounds, 50 rounds of belted ammunition for the team RPD, and a B-25 radio—this has a high frequency with virtually unlimited range; and a simple antenna which can be thrown over a tree branch. The operator always used Morse code, never voice, in order to save batteries. The third member of the team carried the RPD and 500 rounds of ammunition. The fourth man carried an RPK, seven spare magazines, and 500 rounds for the RPD.

Each team member carried a standard 32 Recce Wing issue Ka-Bar type knife; and a first aid shock pack. The shock pack contained morphine, adrenalin, a suture kit, a plasma drip, paraffin gauze, and one filled water bottle. Each member carried the shock pack in the same location on his webbing belt to ease location by any members of the team in an emergency. The webbing belt was never removed, since it supported the essentials for survival in an ambush: the shock pack, the leader's radio, one water bottle, and ammunition magazines. Team members each carried a rucksack containing a sleeping bag, a 'bivvie' (shelter-half), ration packs (high energy bars or hard biscuits), and ammunition. No changes of clothing were carried. Explosives carried included white phosphorus grenades, used as offensive weapons and for signalling helicopters, and 'bunker bombs'. These latter were a Recce Wing invention, consisting of an emptied hand flare plastic tube filled with a combination of plastic explosive and a slow-burning explosive: a mixture producing an extreme concussion effect far greater than the 'flash and bang' gren-

*The Pro Patria Medal, awarded for service in the Operational Area. The orange ribbon has broad dark blue and narrow white stripes; the yellow metal medal has a dark blue central disc. (Author's photo)*

▶

*A member of 32 Battalion receives the Pro Patria Medal and his lieutenant's pips, 1985. The white tapes on the epaulettes signify an officer candidate. (Paratus Magazine)*

ades used by other countries. The total loads of pack, water, ammunition, radios, and weapon could average 40 kilograms (88 pounds) per man. The unit operated and moved only at night, usually moving in single file.

Other personal and survival equipment was non-standard and improvised by each member. 32 Battalion had in its employ a former member, wounded in action, who became the battalion's tailor and webbing-maker. Uniforms were provided to match those worn by enemy troops in the operational area. All webbing equipment was made from green nylon and canvas material. A specially designed Recce Wing assault vest was developed, whose design was later adopted by other SADF specialist units. Camouflage face veils were provided to keep insects out of the eyes and nose, and for concealment. The white troops would wear the SADF issue black camouflage paint (known as 'black is beautiful' by the troops) over all exposed skin areas at all times while in the Operational Area. Boots were almost exact copies of US issue jungle boots, but made from green and brown canvas with a smooth sole. A canvas sneaker-type boot was also used, with smooth, rounded-edge soles to inhibit tracking.

Though 32 Recce Wing members were jump-qualified the unit never deployed by parachute. Infiltration was made by helicopter to within 15 kilometres of the target, and the teams would then proceed on foot. During the rainy season rubber boats or canoes were occasionally used for infiltration.

When out of the operational area the Recces trained constantly. Each man was cross-trained to perform every member's task, including signalling and medical specialities. Anti-tracking and exfiltration techniques were constantly up-dated and practised in the field. The trick of walking backwards, the heel being placed down first, was natural to the black 'troopies' who had been tracking all their lives, but new to the white troops. Conversely, the white Recce members were more accustomed to using radios. Each member was trained in the use, assembly, and disassembly of all Communist bloc weapons that they might encounter while on operations, from the Makarov pistol to the SAM-7. Demolitions, navigation, bushcraft, advanced medical training, and fire direction training were also up-dated.

The success of the unit was astounding. During the operations of 1978 to 1983, the Recce Wing suffered only four members wounded by enemy fire. The Wing successfully completed all missions, and was never discovered as a SADF unit by either FAPLA or SWAPO. Though highly effective, the unit never officially existed: the SADF denied its existence. No medals for gallantry were received by the unit members; one man was recommended for two medals, which were denied. Only the Pro Patria Medal was awarded to Recce Wing members—a medal routinely received by all SADF troops for service in the border area.

# THE RECONNAISSANCE REGIMENTS

The first Reconnaissance Regiment was founded in Durban on 1 October 1972 as a small, specialized Special Air Service or Selous Scout-type unit capable of operating deep inside enemy territory to obtain valuable intelligence while tracking enemy units. Col. Jan Breytenbach commanded the new unit, designated 1 Reconnaissance Commando or 1 Recce. Elements of this unit were later expanded into additional Recce groups; though termed 'regiments', the Recce groups consist of only small numbers of individuals or 'operators', who are secretive, seldom photographed, and expertly trained.

The current Reconnaissance Regiments include 1 Recce based at Durban in Natal Province; 2 Recce (Citizen Force) based at Voortrekkerhoogte in the Transvaal; 4 Recce based at Langebaan in Cape Province; and 5 Recce based at Phalaborwa in the Transvaal. It is of note that 3 and 6 Reconnaissance Regiments were formed in 1980, at the end of the Rhodesian War, from ex-Selous Scouts and Rhodesian Special Air Service members, but were disbanded in 1981, with all members being absorbed into other Recce units. All regiments are controlled by a headquarters unit located at Voortrekkerhoogte.

The Recces are trained to act in small groups or as individuals with little support. The Recce's mission is to gather covert strategic and tactical intelligence information about enemy activity behind the lines. On occasion they have also participated in special combat operations in enemy rear areas, destroying special targets, and harassing the enemy. Though little information has been officially released, it is known that the Recces normally operate in five- or six-man teams, though references to two-man reconnaissance teams operating inside Angola have been gleaned from official SADF sources. Each member of the team is a specialist in his field. A typical team might consist of a navigator, tracker, medic, demolitions expert, and signaller.

The requirements for applicants for Recce training are stringent. The recruiting literature states that an applicant must be prepared to enlist in the Permanent Force for three years after National Service is fulfilled[1]; must be between 18 and 35 years of age, physically and spiritually fit; must possess appropriate military skills which can be developed; must hold a matric (similar to a US High School diploma), desire to serve their country in a special capacity and seek an outstanding career, be a South African citizen, have no criminal record, and be fluent in English and Afrikaans. The applicant can specialize in a particular field in the Recces including medical, signals, logistics, weapons, diving, handling of boats, demolition, or research and development. It is reported that each year as many as 700 applicants from all branches of the SADF apply for Recce selection and that only 45 candidates are accepted.

Recce candidates are selected from volunteers drawn from all SADF branches. Recruiters visit SADF units to outline in detail, through lecture and film, the requirements, the nature and role of the unit, and the strenuous training programme. Recce training consists of a preselection phase (three days), Special Forces orientation (two weeks), selection (three days), training (42 weeks), and specialization.

*Example of a specially built South African Defence Force Special Forces assault vest with an integral 'hot extraction' rig.* (Paratus *Magazine*)

---

[1] All white South African males are eligible for two years military service when they reach the age of 18. At the end of this commitment they may apply for Permanent Force Membership, and a stay in Special Forces providing an additional three-year commitment is made. If a stay is not requested, service in the Citizen Force or Commando Force must be maintained until the age of 55.

## Training

The pre-selection phase commences with a day of psychological testing. The applicant must undergo a complete medical and psychological examination, and an interview during which he must convince the selection board that he would contribute to the unit and fit in as a team member. After successful completion of the psychological testing an exacting one-day physical test commences. This test includes completing variations of: a 30-kilometre march, wearing all gear and carrying a rifle and 30 kilogram (66 pound) sandbag, within six hours; an eight-kilometre run with rifle and all kit, in 45 minutes; 40 push-ups, eight chin-ups, and 68 sit-ups in a specified time limit; 40 shuttle runs of seven metres each in 90 seconds; and a swim of 45 metres in a specified period. The third day of the pre-selection phase includes a route march. When a candidate satisfactorily completes the pre-selection testing he is then ready for the Special Forces orientation course. This includes two weeks of advanced infantry skills and physical training. The physical training lasts for eight hours each day as a preparation for the selection course. A 20 per cent drop-out rate is experienced during this phase.

The selection process includes three days of survival and bush orientation training. Rations, water and sleep are severely limited. Physical training is continuously practised and testing is frequent. A typical day of testing at this stage could include one hour of calisthenics, no breakfast, a route march during which candidates must identify and remember numerous terrain features, three assault course runs carrying a 35 kilogram (77 pound) pack and an ammunition can filled with cement, and a five-kilometre run. Candidates are evaluated for adaptability, discipline, navigation skills, any fears of animals or situations, care of weapons and equipment, memory, powers of observation, leadership, and movement in the bush. Emphasis is placed on the candidate's ability to work successfully with other candidates while under stress.

The final 42-week training course consists of an individual phase; a basic parachuting course; training in minor tactics (foreign and platoon weapons instruction, survival, urban warfare, and vehicle movement training); water orientation (small boat instruction, basic diving, swimming, and survival); air orientation (static parachute jumping, rapelling, fast roping, forward air control, and helicopter drills); and basic demolitions. The parachute course consists of two phases: physical training and parachute train-

ing. Extensive endurance and body-building training is initially conducted for ten 40-minute periods each day. Speed marches progress from five kilometres up to 25 kilometres with full kit and rifle. A frequent exercise is marching around the parade ground holding the 25 kilogram (55 pound) cement 'marble' above the head. From an average class, by the time the second phase of parachute training is reached 40 to 50 per cent will have dropped out. The Recces make static line jumps from 150 metres and then progress to free-fall jumping, and HALO (High Altitude, Low Opening) jumps.

Navigation techniques are taught and students are expected to navigate through swamps and waterways. Various team-building exercises are held including races and forced marches over sand carrying heavy weights. Teamwork and leadership qualities are watched for by the instructors. Candidates are rated for ability to work under stress, resistance to cold, adaptability, stamina, co-ordination, and general fitness. The candidates are tested frequently for psychological, physical, and psycho-motor

*A member of the Reconnaissance Regiments in training. The operator wears a South African-manufactured copy of a Cuban cap and issue nutria T-shirt and shorts. (South African Defence Force)*

skills, the ability to think when extremely tired and behave well physically while under mental pressure.

A 'crunch' phase of testing begins with a forced march of 38 kilometres. Well into the march the candidates are allowed to fill water bottles, while the instructors try to entice the men to quit the course by offering food or ice-cold soft drinks. When the candidates reach their destination they are given rations that have been made inedible by contamination with diesel fuel. Any added tortures that the instructors can devise are heaped upon the men. Though a gruelling experience for the candidate, their ultimate safety is assured by doctors, training cadre, and psychologists monitoring each step the candidates make. When the last rendezvous point is reached and the candidates think that they can finally rest, a new marching order is given for an additional 30 kilometres. For those candidates who proceed from this point the instructors lie in wait with more offers of food, water, or transport if the candidate will drop out. Other gruelling ordeals await the candidate, ranging from surviving being taken 'prisoner' by Recce cadre dressed as terrorists, to solving mind-boggling puzzles

*A Recce diver in training landing on a beach carrying a folding-stock*

while short of sleep and food and after strenuous forced marches. The candidates who complete this training are now considered qualified 'Operators'. (Candidates who do not pass the pre-selection, special forces orientation, selection, or training phases are remustered, trained, and sent on to one of the other branches of the SADF.)

The Recce is then posted to an existing team and takes a speciality, usually the one he excelled in during training. Specialization could include sniping, urban warfare, free fall, HALO or HAHO parachuting, or team leadership. Besides normal pay depending on rank and additional allowances for parachuting or demolitions course completion, the Recces receive additional operator's pay allowances. Operators are constantly tested and evaluated and must requalify as Operators each year. Recce enlisted men, once they reach the rank of sergeant, may apply to be considered for officer status.

## Operations

The Recces, like many similar units, use specialized and personalized gear and uniforms, and both Western and Communist bloc weapons. Of special interest is the practice of providing the operators with South African-manufactured copies of camouflage uniforms used by other countries, SWAPO, and FAPLA. These uniforms would be worn to blend in with foreign troops when on covert external operations or in the operational zone of South-West Africa.

Recce missions are covert and secretive by definition, and the details of operations are never known to the outside world. In May 1985 a covert mission conducted by a group of nine operators was blown when the Recces were discovered over 2,000 kilometres inside Angola in the oil-rich province of Cabinda. In the fighting that ensued two South Africans were killed and their leader, Capt. Wynand du Toit, captured; the remaining six operators returned to South Africa safely and without incident. Several Angolan troops were also killed or wounded in the action. The official South African account of the 'Cabinda Incident', outlined in the following paragraphs, provides insight into the operational methods used by the Recces:

On 13 May 1985 a South African Navy strike craft carrying the Recce operational and back-up teams left the port of Saldanha Bay and travelled to a point 160 kilometres off the Angolan coast near the Zaire border. The mission was to confirm the existence of African National Congress (ANC) and SWAPO bases in the vicinity of Cabinda; previous intelligence identified this area as containing a major

*AK-47. (South African Defence Force)*

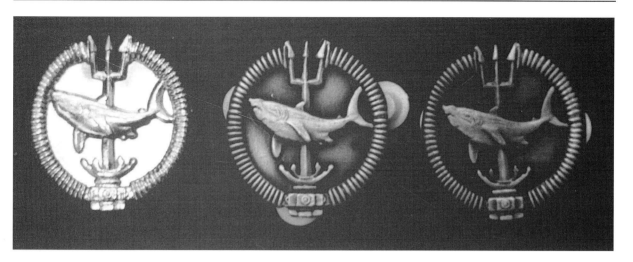

ANC training base from which insurgents were returned to South Africa. The area contains oil storage installations run jointly by the Angolans and the Gulf Oil Company; due to its importance numerous Angolan military bases are situated in the province. Unconfirmed reports had US Vietnam veteran and British ex-SAS men guarding the installations.

The strike craft brought the Recces close to the coast on the night of 19 May. An advance party was launched from the strike craft to gather intelligence on the terrain features of the small beach where the full team would land; the strike craft maintained a holding position while the advance party rowed ashore in rubber dinghies. The beach reconnaissance observed no extraordinary activity in the area, and it was decided to launch the mission the next night. The night of 20 May was dark and cloudy—ideal weather. The Recce team boarded small rubber dinghies for the trip to the coast while the Navy strike craft returned to sea. The team were forced to launch their boats further from the shore than originally planned. The longer journey, combined with seas rougher than those experienced by the advance party, threw off the precise mission timing. As the group approached the shore Capt. du Toit also observed, through a night vision scope, that a small fishing boat was in the immediate area and individuals were on the beach around a small fire. The team waited off-shore until the fishing boat left the area. The rigid timetable for completion of the mission was now almost three hours behind schedule, and the danger of detection grew. After landing on the beach the boats were hidden and a rendezvous point established in case the group had to regroup.

The team climbed a high bluff and followed a route, reconnoitred by the advance party, that skirted a small village and led to a road. The team miscalculated the distance to the road and turned back before reaching it, losing another hour. Du Toit decided to continue with the mission and

reach the lay-over position, or hide, in a densely wooded area within the two remaining hours of darkness. South African intelligence and aerial photographs showed an uninhabited area: in fact, the area the team entered was surrounded by newly constructed, well-camouflaged FAPLA bases. The hide was finally reached at daybreak. Intelligence showed that the hide area contained a dense thicket of jungle ideal for concealment, with a strip of coastal brush that would provide an escape route: in reality, the terrain features had changed and the thicket was cut off from the coastal strip of jungle growth. The team was now in an island of dense growth.

The team went to ground in the hide and formed an all-round defensive position, with one man in an observation post several metres to the north with a view of the course they had travelled. At dawn the outline of a well-camouflaged FAPLA base was discovered 1,000 metres from the hide position. Some hours later a small FAPLA patrol was observed following the tracks unavoidably left by the team in the tall, wet grass. This FAPLA patrol withdrew, but returned with a larger patrol which approached and passed the hide. At 1700 hours a three-man FAPLA patrol followed the team's spoor directly to the thicket, and stopped; they examined the tracks that ended short of the thicket, and returned to the base. At this moment a number of FAPLA troops approached the hide from the opposite direction. Heavy incoming fire was aimed at the Recces by an Angolan force only four metres south of their all-around defensive position. With RPG rockets striking around the defensive position, Capt. du Toit gave the order to withdraw.

The only way out was to retrace their route of the night

before. Two Recces were wounded as the team broke out of the thicket. A group of FAPLA troops deployed 50 metres west of the thicket opened fire with RPDs, RPGs, and numerous AK-47s. The Recce team turned and headed north, pursued by large groups of FAPLA soldiers. A third group of FAPLA troops now advanced from the west, and the team was caught in a pincer movement; their only escape lay to the east, where 40 metres of waist-high grass led to a clump of trees. Capt. du Toit and two team members followed a shallow depression through the grass while the rest of the team waited in the thicket. Du Toit's group of three quickly drew all the FAPLA attention and fire, and over 30 FAPLA troops advanced on their exposed position. Cpl. van Breda was killed, while du Toit and Cpl. Liebenberg fought on. Capt. du Toit later estimated that the fighting had ensued for a full 45 minutes (the average bush contact lasted 15 to 30 seconds). By this time both men were short of ammunition and wounded repeatedly. Their position was overrun by the FAPLA troops. Cpl. Liebenberg was dead. Capt. du Toit was badly wounded, but conscious.

A FAPLA soldier turned him over while stripping him of his watch and equipment, realized he was still alive, and shot him through the neck. Still conscious, with wounds in the shoulder, neck, and arm, du Toit was savagely beaten by the group of FAPLA soldiers. Accused of being a mercenary, du Toit informed the frenzied group that he was a South African officer. The Angolans were surprised to have captured a South African soldier, unaware that he was a member of the famed Recces. After much abuse, du Toit

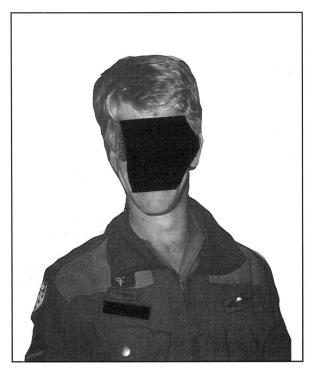

◄

*Snapshot of an anonymous corporal of 7th Medical Battalion wearing the non-standard parachutist's slangvel. The medical qualification badge and free fall parachutist's qualification badge can clearly be seen.*

*A typical load carried by a member of 7th Medical Battalion: (1) Niemoller vest (2) fighting knife (3) 'black is beautiful' camouflage cream (4) wooden spoon (5) collapsible 5-litre water bottle, front view (6) strobe light (7) flashlight/torch (8) Beta light (9) pencil flare projector (10) pencil flares (11) field stove (12) whistle (13) field dressing (14) Bic lighter (15) carabinier (16) collapsible 5-litre water bottle, rear view.*

▼

*Marines practise an amphibious assault in Walvis Bay, 1988.* (Paratus Magazine)

was eventually given medical treatment in Cabinda and taken to the capital, Luanda, where he was put in hospital.

The remaining six Recce operators made their way to the north, regrouped, made contact with the Navy strike craft, and returned to South Africa. The possibility of their presence was totally ignored by FAPLA after they captured Capt. du Toit.

Du Toit was interrogated by the Angolans, who maintained that the Recce group intended to destroy the oil refinery; he eventually confessed to this. Accusations from both sides abounded. The South Africans claimed that du Toit was suffering from extreme psychological torture, deprivation, and threats. After 837 days of solitary confinement in an Angolan prison du Toit was involved in a complicated prisoner exchange. This involved the freeing of du Toit and the return of the remains of his two comrades; while a French national, Pierre-Andre Albertini

(jailed in Ciskei on terrorism charges), a Dutch national, Klaas de Jonge, and 170 FAPLA prisoners held by UNITA, were freed by the South Africans.

\* \* \*

Due to the recent political developments in South Africa and the government reconciliation with the African National Congress and other groups, Special Forces as a branch of service was disbanded on 31 March 1992. The Reconnaissance Regiments now fall, in a limited form, directly under the Chief of the Army.

The individual Recce operator is undoubtedly one of the most highly trained and specialized individuals in the SADF, and on a par with any foreign special forces soldier. As a unit, the Recces hold a reputation for the successful completion of military operations in Southern Africa carried out in the presence of expertly trained and equipped Cuban, East German, and Soviet advisors.

# OTHER SADF AND POLICE UNITS

### 7th Medical Battalion Group

The 7th Medical Battalion Group, or 7 Med, provides medical support to the Special Forces, the Parachute Battalions, the Intelligence Division, and the South African Police Task Force. This specially trained unit is also tasked with research and instruction in chemical warfare, combat techniques, field medical techniques, and parachute training.

The South African Medical Service was organized in July 1979 as the fourth SADF service along with the Army, Air Force and Navy; it has headquarters in Pretoria, with regional Medical Commands controlling the three military hospitals located in Pretoria, Cape Town, and Bloemfontein, as well as the medical services located at most military installations. The SAMS is also responsible for the examination of all National Servicemen prior to induction, disaster relief operations, the maintenance of medical services to military dependents, the provision of medical ser-

*South African Marines in hand grenade training, 1988. All wear the Pattern 1983 nylon ammunition vest.* (Paratus *Magazine*)

vices to the poorer population of South Africa, and veterinary support to the SADF and the local population. All 7 Med specific training is conducted through the Training Command at the SAMS Training Centre and College.

The importance of the 7 Med operational medical orderly, or 'field medic', and doctors of the SAMS cannot be overstated. The time factor is crucial when attending to wounded on the modern battlefield, since 90 per cent of fatalities occur within the first 60 minutes after being wounded. In a combat situation, each soldier is trained and capable of providing first aid to a comrade. This 'buddy aid' assists the wounded soldier by stopping bleeding and immobilizing the patient until a field medic can arrive on the scene. The field medic then stabilizes the soldier for eventual casevac to a hospital. Transport usually consists of a flight in a Puma helicopter with a doctor present; en route to the scene the doctor maintains constant radio contact with the field medic and is briefed on the patient's injury. The doctor advises the field medic as to what additional medical support is needed, and relays medical information to the hospital to enable the doctors and staff to prepare operating rooms in preparation for surgery. Once the patient is on board the Puma the doctor continues needed treatment until the hospital is reached.

The SAMS ratio is one doctor to one company of

*Marines disembarking from a Puma helicopter during assault training, 1988.* (Paratus *Magazine*)

troops. In areas where the troops are highly dispersed or the distances great a ratio of one doctor to thirty troops is maintained. The goal—usually achieved—is that a wounded man reach a doctor's care within 20 minutes. The field medic is trained in 'buddy aid' procedures and other techniques including administering saline drips, anaesthesia, and minor surgical procedures. The training of the typical 7 Med doctor includes civilian medical training; advanced emergency situation training; and the completion of a military medical course that includes the treatment of high velocity and explosive injuries, shock and trauma.

## South African Corps of Marines

South African naval units have a long, but disrupted, history of service ashore with the mission of harbour defence. In 1885 the Natal Naval Volunteers manned naval guns to defend Durban. It was not until the Second World War that the first South Africans were to truly become Marines, however, when 78 men were seconded to the British Royal Marines, serving with distinction throughout the war.

On 1 May 1946 the South African Naval Forces were reconstituted as the Union Defence Forces. At this time the Navy consisted of 60 officers, 806 other ranks, three frigates, two boom defence vessels, one minelayer, and eleven motor launches. By 1951 the Navy had grown to 132

officers, 1,500 other ranks, with the addition of two minesweepers, two destroyers, and a survey vessel. The South African Naval Forces became the South African Navy. One outcome of this naval expansion was that the South African Corps of Marines was officially formed in 1951 around the nucleus of the Royal Marine Second World War veterans. At that time the role of the Marines was the coastal, anti-aircraft, and radar defence of port installations, strategic points, and coastal areas; and also providing light anti-aircraft artillery for South African forces in the field.

In 1955 South Africa and the United Kingdom signed the Simonstown Agreement, under which South Africa would purchase British-made ships in exchange for the transfer of the Royal Navy's Simonstown naval base and dockyard to South Africa. The provisions of this agreement were fulfilled on 2 April 1957. At this time the South African Navy moved the main naval base from Durban and headquarters from Pretoria to Simonstown. With the expansion of the Navy the future of the Marines seemed assured; but in 1955, when the Soviet Union equipped its ships with guided missile launchers, the usefulness of coastal artillery (and with it the Corps of Marines) seemed to have disappeared. Consequently, the South African Corps of Marines was disbanded on 1 October 1955, the coastal artillery and radar units being transferred to the Navy.

Subsequently it was believed that a potential terrorist threat to South African harbours and coastal regions provided a need for a Corps of Marines with a mission similar to that of the volunteer naval parties of the 1880s. In June 1980 the South African Corps of Marines was revived as a branch of the South African Navy, with the mission of protecting harbours, naval installations, and rivers against sabotage. An amphibious assault capability was also maintained. The majority of the Corps are Permanent Force members and operate closely with the South African Police. Half of the annual draft of National Servicemen into the South African Navy are destined to become Marines.

The Marine's training is comprehensive and includes

*Marines undergoing rifle grenade instruction. Note the front and rear of the Pattern 1983 nylon ammunition vest, and the ballistic helmet with nutria cover. (Paratus Magazine)*

both naval and infantry skills. A six-week basic naval training course is offered at SAS *Saldanha* which includes diving and amphibious operations. After completion of the naval segment of training the Marines move on to a 24-week infantry course; this includes intensive training at Eikeboshock in physical fitness, weapons familiarization, bushcraft, tactics, unarmed combat, hygiene, and drilling. The next phases include signalling, conventional warfare, and counter-insurgency training. This course is almost identical to that undertaken by South African Army trainees. Other similarities to the Army include uniforms and field gear, which are standard SADF issue. A final exercise is conducted in the Touws River area. After graduation, a period of duty along the South-West Africa/Angola border was the rule in the 1980s. Upon completion of duty in the Operational Area the Marines would crew Harbour Protection Boats (HPBs). These locally manufactured boats, of the Namacurra Class, are twin-hulled, 9.5 metres long, fast and manoeuvrable. Each has a crew of five, mounts machine guns and 20mm cannon, and has radar and other state-of-the-art electronic equipment.

With peace in South-West Africa, the South African internal reforms, the end of the Cold War, and economic

strains and reductions in defence spending, the mission of the Marines was in doubt, and the Corps was again disbanded on 18 January 1990.

## SADF Divers

The South African Navy diving branch was started in 1941 at the Louw-Halvors Dock in Cape Town. By 1942 a team of salvage divers was operating in the Mediterranean from HMS *Gamtoos*. By the end of the war there were two South African diver teams in operation. Only one of the war-trained divers, PO W.S.P.Lingenfelder, remained active after the war; but he was instrumental in the development of the Diving Division. On 14 October 1953 the minelayer SAS *Skilpad* sank at Salisbury Island, and PO Lingenfelder was the only qualified diver available to help salvage the vessel. In the face of this obvious need the Navy quickly initiated plans and funding to provide a diving school, and in September 1954 the first Navy diving and salvage course was offered. With the signing of the Simonstown Agreement the South African Navy officially opened a diving school there on 1 July 1957, followed by the addition of a decompression chamber in 1958, and a ten-metre tank and 33-foot diving tower in 1965. New diving units were established at SAS *Donkin* in Port Elizabeth, SAS *Inkonkoni* in Durban, and SAS *Port Rex* in East London.

The diver's mission is mine clearance, the protection of shipping and harbour installations against terrorist or sabotage, underwater salvage or repairs, and assisting in the berthing of naval vessels in dry dock. The divers are trained at the SAS *Simonsberg* Diving School at Simonstown. The diving school candidate must possess a matric, and pass swimming, psychological, and medical examinations. He must attend an eleven-week diving course to qualify for air scuba diving. The first three weeks involve extensive physical training; a typical morning includes group circuits, a 12-kilometre run, a one-mile 'fin' or swim wearing complete wetsuit and gear, a run up steps wearing the wetsuit and carrying sandbags, 'buddy' exercises in which the men take turns carrying each other, or completing sit-ups with logs held to their chests. The afternoon exercises include dives in full kit, with air tanks, to a depth of

*Marines undergoing rifle grenade instruction. The officer's winter 'step-out' dress and the front of the Pattern 1983 nylon ammunition vest can be seen. (Paratus Magazine)*

*Gen. P.J.Coetzee visits Koevoet. The distinctive rubberized shoulder flashes and the SWAPOL beret badge are worn. (South African Police)*

40 metres. Upon completion of the Part 1 Diver's Course the trainees receive their diving badge, marking their qualification to dive to a depth of 36 metres using scuba gear and surface air supply lines. The divers also attend a short fire-fighting course, before being sent to sea for 12 to 18 months. The diver is subsequently posted to the Naval Diving Section for duty along South Africa's coast. After four years' service the Part 2 or Part 3 Diving Courses are also available: these train divers to increase their depth capability to 54 metres on air and gas mixtures, standard or 'hard hat' diving.

A recent operation in which the divers participated involved the rescue of passengers stranded on the tour ship *Oceanus*, which foundered and sank off the Transkei coast on 5 August 1991. The divers were notified of the situation on 4 August 1991 at 0215 hours, quickly left Cape Town by helicopter, and reached The Haven, a seaside resort on the Transkei coast to be used as a base of operations. A group of four divers arrived on the foundering ship at 0900 hours with orders to locate 21 passengers who were not accounted for (it was later learned that these passengers had been rescued earlier by small boats and were already ashore). The four divers, all based at the Diving School, were awarded the Honoris Crux, South Africa's highest award for bravery.

## South-West African Police Counter-Insurgency Unit (SWAPOL-TIN)

The South-West African Police Counter-Insurgency Unit (SWAPOL-TIN), nicknamed 'Operation K' or more familiarly 'Koevoet', were initially little known outside the Operational Area. This predominantly black unit accounted for one third of SWAPO casualties suffered in the fighting along the South-West Africa/Angolan border between 1978 and 1988.

In 1966, when SWAPO terrorist activities were initiated, South African Police units were the first to respond to the threat, which they had almost eliminated within three years, using standard police and counter-insurgency tactics. After two years spent rebuilding its military structure at bases in Zambia SWAPO resumed small-scale terrorist activities. When the Portuguese withdrew from Angola in 1975 SWAPO escalated its level of operations, infiltrating from Angola into northern South-West Africa. In response the South African government transferred responsibility for the security of South-West Africa to the Army, with police units reducing their participation in the fighting.

In 1978 Gen. Malan, Chief of the South African Defence Force (SADF), approached the SAP with plans for establishing a special counter-insurgency unit. Maj. Gen. Johannes 'Sterk Hans' Dreyer, a counter-insurgency warfare expert, travelled to South-West Africa to develop an expanded police role against terrorism. Using experience gained during South African Police participation in the

1: Trainee, Parachute School, 1979
2: Paratrooper, 44 Para Bde., 1990
3: Captain, 44 Para Bde., 1989
4: Brig. M.J.Du Plessis; Cassinga, 1978

A

1: Pathfinder, 44 Para Bde., 1982
2: Private, Hunter Group, 1968
3: Private, Hunter Group, 1968

B

1: Trooper, 32 Battalion, 1987
2: Lieutenant, 32 Bn., 1985
3: Capt., 32 Bn. Recce Wing, 1983
4: Sgt. Maj. Rogers, 32 Bn., 1990

C

1: Special Forces
   Operator, 1982
2: Recce Operator, 1987
3: Recce Operator, 1984

D

1: Recce Operator/Instructor, 1989
2: Maj. Du Toit, 1987
3: Col, Jan Breytenbach, 1990

E

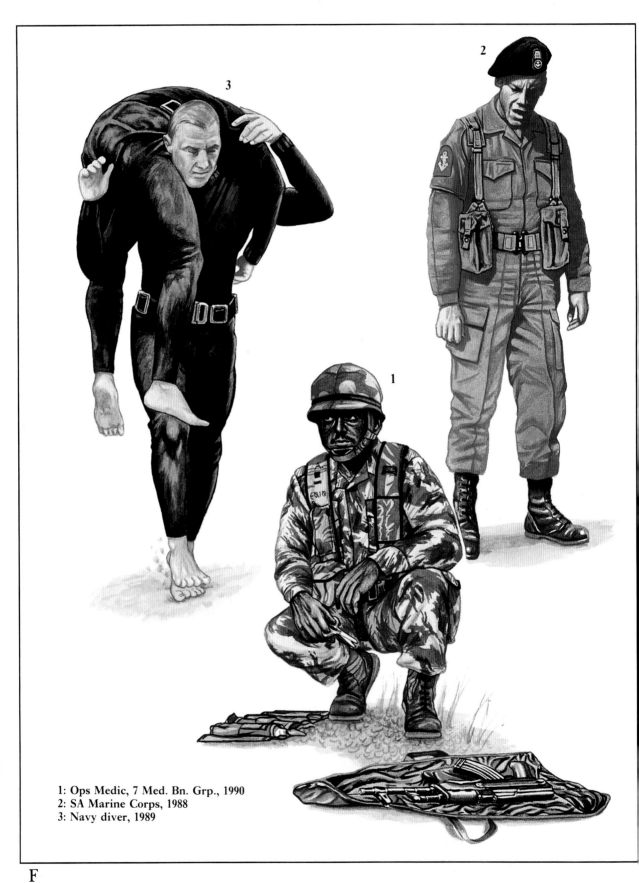

1: Ops Medic, 7 Med. Bn. Grp., 1990
2: SA Marine Corps, 1988
3: Navy diver, 1989

F

1: Constable, Koevoet, 1987
2: Special Constable, Koevoet, 1985
3: SAP Task Force (Koevoet), 1984

G

1: Constable, SARP STF, 1985
2: Staff Sgt, SARP RTF, 1985
3: Constable, SAP COIN; Rhodesia, 1969

H

'Wings' - see text commentary for identification

I

J

Insignia - see text commentary for identification

'Koevoet' insignia - see text commentary for identification

'Koevoet' insignia - see text commentary for identification

Rhodesian War, Dreyer envisioned the formation of a Selous Scout-type unit recruited from local men who knew the customs, language, and terrain. At this time the police were engaged in developing a guard force to provide security for Ovambo headmen and politicians threatened by SWAPO. After discussions with local Ovambo leaders—the largest tribal group in the area—several constables were suggested as likely candidates for the unit. These men were recruited, sent out to recruit others, and formed SWAPOL-TIN as an extension of routine police security operations in June 1979. This group underwent training at the Special Constable School near Ondangwa, and became the first SWAPOL-TIN fighting group, Zulu Foxtrot. With little help from headquarters, Dreyer concentrated on training, developing tactics, establishing an intelligence network, and gathering equipment. Zulu Foxtrot consisted of ten Security Policemen and 64 locally recruited Special Constables, skilled in weapons and tracking, combined to form a group providing quick exploitation of intelligence material and a ready response to the identification of tracks in the course of day-to-day operations; a further goal was the infiltration and destruction of SWAPO's well-established intelligence system.

The first unit success occurred in May 1979. A group of 12 terrorists infiltrated the white farming area south-east of the Etosha Game Reserve and bayoneted to death a number of civilians, including women and children. The Army moved into the area but had difficulty locating the terrorists. Dreyer convinced the Army to give his unit an opportunity to track the terrorists. The spoor was quickly picked up by 23 Ovambo trackers and one white, and followed for seven days until contact was made. This successful operation established Dreyer's unit concept and formulated the tactics and logistical aspects to be used by the unit. Now a proven commodity, two additional fighting groups were authorized.

SWAPOL-TIN's success rate grew to 50 to 80 kills a month, though they still operated with outdated equipment with little outside support or recognition. After pleading his case to headquarters in Pretoria, Dreyer's funding for SWAPOL-TIN or 'Koevoet' was expanded.

*An aerial photograph of Koevoet on the spoor. The trackers are closing in on the terrorists with the remainder of the unit standing by in preparation for the contact. A helicopter would not normally be present. (South African Police)*

*A Koevoet unit prepares to leave Oshakati for an operation in the bush, 1981. The second model Police Casspir is in use, distinguished by the fold-down door immediately in front of the side windows. (South African Police)*

Three Hippo armoured personnel carriers (the predecessor to the Casspir) were sent to the unit. After an initial lack of enthusiasm for the carriers, the first incident involving the use of two Hippos resulted in 18 dead terrorists. It was then decided to utilize all vehicles while developing the unit into a highly mobile and heavily armed hunter-killer team.

Extensive experimentation in tactics and weapons led to each group being organized with 40 Ovambo and four whites in four Casspir APCs with one Blesbok mine-protected supply vehicle in support. Dreyer requested unlimited freedom of movement throughout the Operational Area for his unit; and after much discussion with the Army, Koevoet fighting groups were allowed to use hot pursuit tactics anywhere in the OA. Support was initially provided by a small 'fire force' from the Reconnaissance Regiments. The great distances travelled degraded the Recces' response time, however, forcing Koevoet to form its own fire force in early 1980. This fire force, operating on foot, was supported by a Para Brigade quick reaction force.

By 1985 there were three units located at Kaokoland, Kavango, and Ovambo. Each unit controlled a platoon-strength fighting group and an attached intelligence element which conducted supporting operations. A central headquarters, located at Oshakati, provided overall control. Group deployment was to the area where they were most needed. Each group was organized with four Casspir APCs, each carrying up to ten men; a Duiker mine-protected fuel truck; and a Blesbok mine protected supply truck. An individual group was commanded by an officer

or warrant officer while each section was commanded by a sergeant. The second-in-commands of the sections were Special Sergeants or Warrant Officers who had distinguished themselves on operations. Weapons included R-4 and R-5 5.56mm rifles, FN MAGs, AK-47s, US M-79 grenade launchers, and 60mm mortars. Each vehicle was fitted with a combination of .30 and .50 calibre machine guns.

All white members of Koevoet were volunteers with previous experience in either the South African or South-West African Police. Completion of a counter-insurgency course was required before provisional acceptance into Koevoet. A gruelling, realistic selection course, which often led to contacts with insurgents, was then required. Upon completion of selection the new members were required to stay with the unit for two years, though it was not uncommon for group leaders and car commanders to stay with the unit for five years. Transfer out of Koevoet was left up to the individual. Black Koevoet personnel were recruited from the police forces in the Operational Area, with promotions based on individual effectiveness in the field. The fighting groups consisted of men from both Ovambo and Kavango tribes, this tribal mixing providing men familiar with the customs, dialect, and terrain of each area for any operation. Unit cohesion, morale, and experience were maintained by the practice of keeping the fighting groups intact as long as possible. Strength was maintained by adding new recruits rather than by disbanding and reforming the units. The recruits received continuous on-the-job training, paired with experienced men, and were given three weeks' training before being deployed in the Operational Area.

Groups could operate in the bush for one to two weeks at a time, freely ranging the Operational Area looking for spoor. If necessary, additional units were attached for support. Usually the units spent one week in the bush and one week at the base camp resting, training, and maintaining equipment.

Intelligence information gleaned from the local population was extremely important; spoor alone could not be relied on when tracking insurgents, unless it was followed directly after a contact or incident. When following spoor the Koevoet trackers walked or ran, with the rest of the group following closely in the Casspirs. If the spoor was lost the trackers were joined by others from the Casspirs who spread out into a line and continued walking until the spoor was found again. If the spoor was not regained additional information was sought from the local population, and the hunt resumed. The trackers scouting in front of the unit were the first to make contact with any insurgents they encountered. One or two vehicles would provide immediate support and assault the enemy, with the remaining two vehicles staying in reserve or continuing on the track of other insurgents, if any. Upon contact, the logistic vehicles would immediately withdraw to the rear and establish their own security. The attacking Casspirs would circle the contact area at speed while laying down maximum firepower. When all resistance ceased, the unit cordoned off the surrounding area and searched for insurgents who may have separated from the group.

On occasion Koevoet units were ambushed by the insurgent group. If the spoor gave any indication of a large group of insurgents massing for an ambush, the tactic used was for the trackers to withdraw to the relative safety of the Casspirs and track from their protection. Any ambush was handled with the Casspirs performing a mechanized infantry assault. If the insurgent ambush was sprung before the trackers could return to the Casspirs, the trackers would quickly withdraw from the contact and wait out the action, forming an ambush line to stop any insurgents fleeing the area.

Each group adopted a specialized shoulder flash and T-shirt depicting the unit emblem; the emblem (a scorpion, snake, badger, eagle, tiger, etc.) was usually depicted with a broken insurgent AK-47. The unit members wore the uniform of their parent organization. It was not uncommon to see green South-West African Territorial Force uniforms alongside tan and brown South African Police camouflage, brown South African Defence Force and camouflage South-West African Police uniforms. Later in their operations Gen. Dreyer ordered that all members should wear green uniforms.

*Koevoet during a fire-and-manoeuvre exercise. The members have reversed their caps to show the orange day-glo lining for easy air recognition. (South African Police)*

*South-West African Police reservists on parade in the Windhoek area. All wear the distinctive SWAPOL camouflage uniform and cap with back flap. (South African Police)*

The unit's reputation as efficient killers grew, and with it the anti-Koevoet obsession of SWAPO. One legend that arose from the ranks of Koevoet was that of 30-year-old Frans Conradie. In 1981 Conradie and his unit, operating in northern South-West Africa along the Angolan border, accounted for the deaths of 99 SWAPO insurgents. In 1982 his unit, consisting of less than 30 men operating from six vehicles, accounted for 60 dead infiltrators; and another 40 were killed by the unit in the first nine months of 1983, with many others captured. Conradie was never seriously wounded in battle even though he participated in over 140 contacts. He did receive an AK round between the ribs, but was saved from injury when the round struck an ammunition magazine in his Soviet-style chest webbing. Frans accounted for the death of at least 300 enemies in his fighting career. Long-serving South African Army personnel in the Operational Area could not claim anything approaching his fighting record.

Frans started his career in the South African Police and volunteered for duty with one of the first SAP units sent to Rhodesia. He learned his lessons there, and then asked to be transferred to the South African 1 Reconnaissance Regiment. Frans passed the selection course and stayed with the Recces for five years while earning senior jump, free fall, and HALO qualifications. He did see action, though details remain classified. Frans was subsequently approached by Gen. Dreyer and asked to join his new specialist unit.

Frans Conradie moulded his small band into a group of élite counter-insurgency warfare specialists through his detailed operational planning and precise execution of operations. He was unstoppable, calm under fire, detail-orientated—and when going into battle he would play classical music at full volume! In building his group's effectiveness he used his knowledge of tactics, his personnel management skills, and his sense of humour (earning the nickname of 'Smiley Conradie'). His personality was magnetic, and his men would follow him anywhere. He was one of the finest trackers in the Operational Area, and could follow a spoor for days on the ground; he was known to cover 50km at a time in difficult terrain. He could tell the freshness of the spoor, how much weight the man was carrying, if he was tired, wounded, or fresh.

One of Frans Conradie's most impressive feats occurred in July 1983, when he was following the spoor of three terrorists. For three days on foot and running, dressed only in shorts and running shoes, he followed their trail toward the Angolan border until the three split up. He then followed one spoor until he caught up with the man and killed him. He then returned to the point of the 'bombshell' and started tracking the second man, with the same results; and then the third man, who met the same fate.

Frans set many records in the Operational Area. He was the only policeman ever to have called in an air strike in support of operations; this killed a group of 15 insurgents who were putting up stiff resistance. On five separate occasions he personally killed groups of ten men at a time with the modified Hispano-Suizo 20mm cannon that he had mounted on his Casspir. His ruthless effectiveness in the field caused SWAPO to offer a five-figure reward for his elimination. It is ironic that Frans Conradie died not in battle, but in a vehicle accident in September 1983 while returning home from the Operational Area.

SWAPOL-TIN became one of the most successful COIN units in the history of warfare. It was finally disbanded in September 1988, and the South-West Africa Police assumed responsibilities for the area.

## South African Railway Police Special Task Force

The South African Railway Police (SARP) can trace their lineage back to 1867 when a harbour police force was established in Cape Town, consisting of one boat officer and four constables. It was not until May 1916 that a true force with police duties was authorized to protect South African railways and harbours. This force was reorganized on 1 July 1934 as the SARP.

On 24 May 1972 two South Africans of Greek descent hijacked a Boeing 727 and forced the plane to fly to Salisbury, Rhodesia, where landing rights were refused. The plane flew on and landed in Malawi, where it was attacked by the Malawi Army who captured the terrorists. The SARP participation in the episode was limited to conducting an after-action investigation. This incident led to plans to develop a special force to counter such terrorist incidents on South African railways, aircraft, and shipping. This SARP Special Task Force was formed on 24 October 1975; its mission was to resolve hostage situations in buildings, aircraft, ships, and buses throughout South Africa.

Two Task Force combat groups were trained at the SADF Infantry School at Oudtshoorn. The team members were initially trained for rural operations and posted throughout the country along the borders. A core consisting of the commander and instructors were Permanent Force members. In 1980 a Task Force combat group was established for urban operations under the command of Brig. A.F.Horak; its members were trained as snipers, divers, demolition and explosive experts, paratroopers, and

*South African Railway Police Task Force members practise assaulting a hijacked railway coach. (South African Police)*

dog handlers. Initially, only the commander and in-structors were permanent members of the force; the rest of the unit was stationed in other regions of the country, but once a month all members met and conducted exercises and training at their base at Esselen Park. Drills included the forced entering of buildings, climbing up drain pipes, and rappelling from the roofs of buildings to enter through windows. Up to 20 floors of a building were negotiated in training.

The world first learned of the SARP Task Force in 1981 when an Air India Boeing 707 was hijacked by Col. 'Mad Mike' Hoare to extricate a mercenary force from a botched coup attempt in the Seychelles, and flown to Louis

Botha Airport in Durban. The Task Force was deployed around the aircraft while the unit commander negotiated with Col. Hoare; the situation was settled without further incident.

The unit wore their own distinctive pattern of camouflage uniform consisting of a nutria base with splotches of black, dark brown, and green. Of special interest were the camouflage wool berets; and issue trousers with special integral magazine pouches for the Israeli UZI sub-machine gun. The UZI was used extensively by the unit, and figured prominently on their Regional Task Force wing and shoulder flashes, of yellow silk screening on camouflage material.

The unit was disbanded on 1 October 1986 and its members were incorporated into the South African Police, though at lower ranks.

## South African Police Special Task Force

The South African Police Special Task Force is an anti-terrorist force modelled on the British SAS and the German GSG-9. The force is trained to deal with hostage situations, and is based in Pretoria.

In 1975 a terrorist incident occurred that proved the need for such a special police unit. The 'Fox Street incident' occurred on 28 April at the Israeli Consulate on that street in Johannesburg. After a report of shooting at the consular offices two policemen from the Uniform Branch, Constable R.F.Reynders and his partner, arrived at the consulate at 1130 hours to investigate. Upon entering the lobby the officers were met by a young man, Charles Protter, who occupied the lobby reception desk. In response to their inquiries he told them that there had been no shooting, but a female employee's handbag had been stolen. When they asked to interview her they were refused entry into the consulate offices; Protter spoke to another man over the intercom system, who confirmed the story but also denied entry to the officers. The incident was reported to police headquarters. An hour later Detective Sergeant J.Maralich and his team from the Security Branch arrived at the consulate to investigate why telephones there were not being answered. They were met by Protter, who stated that the offices were being redecorated and the telephones were inoperable. While other visitors to the consulate were being denied entry two members of the Police Flying Squad arrived to assist Detective Sergeant Maralich and to investigate a report of terrorist activity at the consulate. A

*SARP Task Force member in full assault uniform. Note the dark Railway Police camouflage uniform with dual Uzi magazine pouches on the trouser leg, Task Force helmet with microphone, armour vest, and gas mask. (South African Police)*

*SARP Regional Task Force members on patrol in a Cape township. The Warrant Officer on the right wears the yellow, silk-screened Task Force emblem of an Uzi sub-machine gun on his camouflage brassard. (M. Sullivan)*

few minutes later a burst of machine gun fire in the street wounded one man and put the police units into operation.

Col. T.Swanepol of the Johannesburg Flying Squad arrived within minutes and took command. Protter was now in the street, moving nervously about while communicating with someone using a small hand-held radio. A great deal of confusion and rumours as to terrorists and multiple killings abounded until the commanding officer of the Security Branch, Maj. Gen. M.Geldenhuys, arrived on the scene at 1400 hours. Geldenhuys quickly took command, cordoned off the surrounding streets, ordered a doctor into the building to treat any wounded, and ordered the arrest of Charles Protter. Protter revealed that there was only one person in the consulate, his brother David. The police began negotiating with David Protter, who immediately threatened to detonate explosives if the police stormed the building, and issued demands. His demands for food and the illumination of the surrounding area were met. By this time, 1700 hours, police snipers were in position. By 1900 hours the Commissioner of the South African Police and the Prime Minister's Security Advisor, Gen. H.J.van den Bergh, arrived in Johannesburg and proceeded personally with the negotiations. Just after midnight David Protter fired another machine gun burst while negotiations continued; but at 0500 hours on 29 April he agreed to give himself up to Gen. van den Bergh. It was learned that David Protter was a security guard at the consulate who had returned to the building to murder his supervisor. He was charged with murder, kidnapping, and the unlawful possession of firearms; found guilty on all

counts; and sentenced to 25 years imprisonment. Charles Protter was charged with kidnapping and the unlawful possession of firearms; found guilty on all counts, he was sentenced to two and a half years in prison.

After this incident the South African Police developed extensive plans to counter terrorism and to prepare for incidents like that at Fox Street, basing their countermeasures on those adopted by other security forces worldwide. The Special Task Force was officially formed in 1976 to deal with urban terrorism, aircraft hijackings, hostage situations, action against armed abductors, assassins, and dangerous mentally disturbed individuals.

Another urban terrorist incident, one of the most dramatic in South African history, was the Silverton Bank Siege. Three men were observed by many citizens, over a period of two days, acting suspiciously, but no reports were officially made to the police. On 25 January 1980 the three men entered the Silverton Branch of the Volkskas Bank in Pretoria, firing AK-47 assault rifles and shouting orders at customers in the crowded bank. The firing was immediately reported to the police, who dispatched the SAP Flying Squad. The Special Task Force was sent to the scene under the command of Brig. B.Wandrag. The Task Force, unobserved by the three armed men, quickly evacuated the numerous occupants of the building to safety. The terrorists issued demands, including the release of Nelson Mandela from prison, and refused negotiation. By this time the area was sealed off. Captain De Swardt of the Task Force conducted negotiations inside the bank, attempting to draw the three men into positions where Task Force snip-

SARP Regional Task Force members keep a watch on crowds in a Cape township *from the top of a Casspir armoured vehicle. (M. Sullivan)*

selection course candidates must serve in the unit for two years. Task Force members continually train to ensure a high standard of efficiency and physical conditioning. The Police Task Force is on permanent stand-by, and elements can be flown to any part of South Africa in little over two hours.

The SAP initially trained specific police units for duty in Rhodesia and the Caprivi Strip, starting in June 1968. All police counter-insurgency training is now conducted at the Maleoskop Counter-Insurgency Training Centre, founded in January 1970. The centre processes over 12,000 police trainees annually.

# THE PLATES

### A1: 'Troopie' in Para School, 1979
The Para School 'troopie' has just completed one of eight jumps on the course at Bloemfontein necessary to earn him his wings. He wears the old style steel helmet with plastic liner which was phased out in 1990; the para model helmet was fitted with a green webbing chin and neck strap. The para smock is a four-pocket, loose-fitting Denison type without a crotch flap. The trousers are khaki drill material with reinforced seat and knees. The jump boots are of British origin; at this early date economics allowed the SADF to purchase their 'jumpers' from foreign sources. The parachute is a standard steerable T-10 type.

### A2: Paratrooper, 44 Para Brigade, Exercise 'Iron Eagle', 1990
The wearing of the nutria *slangvel* parachutist's jump jacket is a characteristic of the South African Paras. The *slangvel* exists in three models, of which the first pattern is shown here. The second pattern is identical but with the addition of a flap over the sleeve pencil pocket. A third variation in a spot camouflage pattern was produced in small numbers and saw limited use. The kevlar-type Israeli para helmet is manufactured under licence in South Africa in both green and brown versions. The helmet is most commonly seen fitted with the nutria cloth cover with its distinctive sun visor.

In 1983 the SADF adopted the nutria Cordura webbing for general issue. The Pattern 83 rucksack, which has an internal frame for support to allow use without the heavy metal outer frame, was issued along with a battle vest and chest webbing. This paratrooper carries the Armscor-manufactured R-4 5.56mm rifle with a 30-round box magazine and Pattern 70 webbing sling. The boots are South African-made 'jumpers'.

ers could get clear shots at them. Unfortunately they were not taken in; and the decision was made to storm the bank. Two terrorists were killed immediately the Task Force entered; the third fired 27 rounds from his AK-47 into the crowd of hostages, wounding six seriously (of whom two later died), before he was himself killed by Task Force members; nine other hostages suffered lesser wounds. The entire assault took less than two minutes.

The requirements for selection into the Task Force are strict: members must be volunteers, over the age of 21, with two years' previous police service, counter-insurgency training, and passes in physical and psychological aptitude tests. The selection process consists of a ten-day basic training course, a two-month probationary period, and a one-year specialized training period. The latter consists of counter-insurgency tactics, hostage situations and rescue operations, VIP or personal protection operations, mountaineering, rappelling, weapons and explosives handling, helicopter insertion, parachuting, and scuba diving. The training is conducted outside Pretoria, with an acceptance rate of 30 per cent. Upon successful completion of the

### A3: Captain, 44 Para Brigade, 1989

In the late 1980s the SADF phased out the 'step-out' uniform for Citizen Force units and adopted a more economical nutria uniform. This officer appears in a variation of the latter. The correct Citizen Force 'step-out' uniform of the Parabats would have the addition of a maroon cravat with the 44 Brigade logo and a pair of white blancoed gaiters worn over the jump boots. The 'snake skin' jump jacket, or *slangvel*, was so nicknamed because of the reinforcing patches on the elbows and pockets; the rip-stop weave gives the appearance of snake skin but is actually grey Pattern 80 webbing material. A South-West African version of the *slangvel* existed which used cloth rather than Pattern 80 material for the reinforcing patches, and had no crotch flap.

The 44 Brigade Headquarters shoulder flashes and the captain's rank slip-ons are made from a rubberized nutria cloth with screen printed devices, known as 'Tupperware' by the troops. This officer wears metal free fall instructor wings pinned through his cloth embroidered wing sewn onto the uniform. The stable belt is maroon nylon fastened with a dull brass buckle with the 44 Para Brigade badge in the centre. The beret is standard para issue with the 44 Para Brigade badge, and the coloured speciality bar, or 'balkie', denoting an infantry soldier. Around the left shoulder he wears the instructor's cord.

### A4: Brigadier M.J.Du Plessis, Cassinga, 1978

Brigadier Du Plessis wears the British Model 1941 para helmet; although rare within the Parabats, the helmet did see limited use, almost exclusively among officers. It was not uncommon to see the helmet covered with hessian and green netting.

### B1: Pathfinder, 44 Para Brigade, 1982

The use of Special Forces equipment was not always a matter of standard issue or personal choice but often of what was available. This Pathfinder wears the standard issue Pattern 70 webbing equipment, with the addition of an Israeli grenade pouch on his belt, over the Para-Fox chest webbing. In 1980 a rucksack was manufactured for Special Forces by a South African hiking equipment company; this did not have an official designation but became known as the Para-Fox. Apart from small differences, like the butterfly frame, the rucksack was made from the same lightweight nylon as the Para-Fox chest webbing. The

Para-Fox rucksack did not have the ripstop design of the Pattern 80 equipment. Because the Para-Fox rucksack appeared in service at roughly the same time as the Pattern 80 equipment (see Plate D1) it was often mistakenly referred to as Pattern 80.

Many of the original Pathfinders preferred the one-piece nutria overall for ease of use. Boots, T-shirt, toggle rope, and net scarf are all standard SADF issue items. This Pathfinder has chosen to use the scarf as a sweatband.

### B2: Private, Hunter Group, 1968

In 1960 the SADF designed a new webbing set based on the British Pattern '44 system; released the following year, it was designated Pattern 61. This webbing was later modified and improved in 1962, 1963, and finally in 1964, when it was re-designated Pattern 61/64 equipment. This Hunter Group private wears one of the earlier versions of the Pattern 61/64 equipment that includes a large pack, com-

*SARP Special Task Force member prepares to arm a stun grenade during a mock attack against terrorists. Note the special helmet with microphone, and dark Railway Police camouflage uniform. The gas mask is used without a filter while in training.* (Paratus Magazine)

pass pouch, and the wider magazine pouches. Many sets of Pattern 61/64 equipment were later donated by South Africa to Rhodesia as war aid. This private wears the first pattern Hunter Group camouflage jacket, trousers, and unusual cap, which were all privately purchased. His ochre coloured jump boots were made in the United Kingdom; and his rifle is a South African R-1, 7.62mm, with a 20-round box magazine.

### B3: Private, Hunter Group, 1968

Hunter Group training was voluntary and uniforms were privately purchased. There is reference to numerous members wearing British DPM camouflage, while at least one man wore the US issue ERDL 1968 Pattern camouflage jungle uniform; but the Hunter Group Pattern 1 and Pattern 2 (shown here) were predominant. Two winter variations of the Pattern 2 uniform had lighter colours. The

*South African Police preparing to enter Alexandria township during the riots of 1976. The man closest to the camera carries a Federal tear gas gun, the man behind him an Israeli-made FN FAL with a tear gas launcher attached. (South African Police)*

Hunter Group pattern jackets had two slanted internal upper pockets and two button-down, lower patch pockets. A soft reinforced padding protected the elbows and trousers knees.

Scarves were an affection popular with the Hunter Group; this private wears the green/orange and brown Rhodesian net type. Webbing equipment was generally the SADF Pattern 61/64; the shape and design of the magazine pouches allowed them to be used for a variety of weapons. The boots are the early SADF model with two buckles on the upper portion; they were similar to the Rhodesian model but less sturdy. The R-1 rifle with Pattern 61/64 sling was standard issue to the Hunter Group.

### C1: Trooper, 32 Battalion, 1987
The largest variation of Special Forces webbing equipment in field service occurred in 32 Battalion. It was not uncommon to see no two members of a company equipped entirely alike. The South African-manufactured nylon DPM camouflage assault vest was a rare find; its origin, and that of the DPM rucksack, is obscure. Both saw limited, short-term use in the battalion. This trooper wears the 32 Battalion summer pattern camouflage shirt and trousers but, as so often, does not have the matching headgear; he has substituted the 32 Battalion winter pattern 'Bigeard' or Kico cap. The trooper carries the R-4 5.56mm rifle with a 35-round magazine and the Pattern 70 sling. The boots are standard SADF issue.

### C2: Lieutenant, 32 Battalion, 1985
A large variety of prototype webbing equipment was field-tested by 32 Battalion. It seemed to be pre-ordained that whatever piece of equipment worked for the battalion in the field was rendered virtually useless after it had been 'improved' and redesigned at the factory during production. In one instance a new issue of rucksacks disintegrated after one day in the field.

This young officer wears the South African-manufactured DPM camouflaged nylon chest webbing, modified with the addition of a holster; green Cordura-type two-litre water bottles; and binocular pouches on his Pattern 80 belt. The shirt and trousers are in 32 Battalion winter pattern camouflage, and the Kico cap in 32 Battalion summer pattern camouflage. He holds an Eastern Bloc manufactured AK-47, as often used on operations in southern Angola, and wears smooth-soled Rhodesian 'Clandestine' boots.

### C3: Captain, 32 Battalion Reconnaissance Wing, 1983
Though most Special Forces equipment was personalized by the user, this Special Forces operator wears an unusual combination of uniform items. Much of his equipment has been 'procured' in the age-old tradition of soldiers throughout the world, or by private purchase, including trading. He wears a standard issue US Marine Corps leaf pattern (ERDL 1968 pattern) 'boonie hat' and Ka-Bar knife (the knife was used by the 32 Recce Wing for a num-

*South African Police COIN unit members in training. Both carry R1 (FN FAL) rifles and wear first pattern camouflage caps and second pattern camouflage shirts and trousers. (South African Police)*

ber of years). The face veil is made from a fine, stretch mesh that was issued to units in large rolls; the desired length was cut and sewn for various camouflage needs including covering kit items, face veils, or bivvie bags. On the rear of the belt an SADF Pattern 1980 butt pack and radio pouch are worn. Braces and webbing belt, map pouch, and 'escape and evasion' three-slot pouch worn on the left hip, are made from nylon and were originally developed by 1 Recce. The escape and evasion pouch usually contained one extra rifle magazine, oil bottle and cleaning kit, emergency rations, and any other items deemed essential by the operator. In an emergency the rucksack was discarded, and only the rifle and the items on the webbing belt were retained to 'run' with.

The gloves are standard South African Air Force issue dabbed with 'black is beautiful' camouflage cream. The boots are SADF Special Forces jungle type, similar to US issue but with a smooth sole to inhibit tracking. A so-called officer's version of these boots existed with soft goatskin leather replacing the webbing on the sides. The camouflage uniform is an early SADF pattern on which 32 Battalion based their winter and summer patterns. Although not produced after 1976, this pattern was adopted by the Recce Wing; old stocks were used, and there was a pronounced difference in dye lots between uniform items. The jacket has four front patch pockets and two internal pockets with vertical zippers.

### C4:  Sergeant-Major Mike Rogers, Pomfret, 1990
Often understrength and undersupplied, 32 Battalion saw more deployments and accounted for more enemy losses than any other unit in the South African security forces. With over 12 years' service, Sgt.Maj. Rogers is the longest serving member of the battalion. Here he wears the official 32 Battalion beret made from first pattern South African Police camouflage material. In the early 1980s new members of the battalion arriving at Buffalo Base found that there were no material stocks available for the making of berets; undaunted, they procured what they could from nearby friendly units. It was not uncommon to see the beret in second pattern SAP camouflage. A beret also exists made from 32 Battalion summer camouflage, but whether this was made for field use or used as an alternative to the official beret is not known. In Pomfret the uniform of the day is nutria, and Sgt.Maj. Rogers wears the short sleeve version of the shirt with the 32 Battalion and Headquarter Company 'Tupperware' shoulder flashes and snap-on rank badges. The black and white cravat and nylon stable belt both sport the 32 Battalion buffalo head badge with the words 'Proelio Procusi' on a scroll beneath.

### D1:  Special Forces Operator, 1982
Typically blacked-up with camouflage cream, this operator employs anti-tracking techniques by removing his Special Forces issued anti-tracking overshoes and exposing the smooth soles of his jungle boots. Ideally this would be done at a water hole or path crossing where pursuit would become confused in the mass of footprints left by local inhabitants and their cattle.

Released for issue in small numbers, Pattern 80 webbing

*A scene from the Silverton Bank Siege, where two hostages were killed: the first action where the SAP Task Force was utilized. The Task Force Warrant Officer on the right wears the seldom-seen Task Force camouflage beret and Maleoskop flash on the camouflage brassard. (South African Police)*

equipment sets were untraceable, durable, and functional for Special Forces personnel. The sets allowed individuals to attach various pouches in different positions as required, distributing their various personal loads. Made from waterproof Pattern 80 material, the vest proved too hot in the extreme temperatures of South-West Africa and Angola. The majority of the Pattern 80 webbing sets were destroyed by the SADF in the mid- to late 1980s. Tucked behind the Special Forces Pattern 80 grenade pouch is a container of Sosagen, which contains a single syringe of locally made but untraceable morphine substitute.

Due to the lack of regular supply and size differences in captured uniforms, Special Forces were forced to manufacture their own copies of Eastern Bloc and African camouflage. This operator wears a pair of South African-manufactured Cuban 'elm leaf' trousers. Each camouflage copy was manufactured in sets which included a shirt, trousers, two types of jackets, three types of headgear, shorts, and a T-shirt. Here the T-shirt is in the East German 'falling rain' pattern. Rather than camouflage their hands with cream many operators choose to wear

*South African Police COIN unit members on duty in Rhodesia. All members wear Rhodesian pattern camouflage uniforms and khaki puttees over short boots. (South African Police)*

gloves; calfskin pilot's gloves were the preferred choice. In a further attempt to blend in with the indigenous population in a clandestine role this operator wears a strip of animal skin around his head as a sweatband.

### D2: Recce Operator, 1987

When working ahead of conventional forces on large-scale cross-border operations Recce operators often choose to wear the nutria field uniform to avoid mistaken identification as the enemy. This operator is in close enough contact with his own forces to feel secure in wearing camouflage, but as a safety measure he has not blacked up with camouflage cream. He wears a combination of Portuguese camouflage trousers and an Egyptian camouflage jacket with two patch pockets—both South African-manufactured Special Forces copies. Over his uniform he wears the South-West

*A South African Police COIN unit member, with AKM, somewhere in South-West Africa. The first pattern police camouflage uniform is worn. (South African Police)*

machine guns. This operator carries an Eastern Bloc manufactured RPK machine gun utilizing the sling from an RPG. The belt and braces are of South African Special Forces origin based on a US design. The RPK 75-round drum pouches are of Eastern Bloc manufacture. The operator wears South African Special Forces manufactured copies of a Libyan camouflage jacket with vertical zippered pockets, French camouflage trousers, and Russian bush hat. Many ex-members of the Rhodesian Security Forces joined South African Special Forces in the early 1980s, contributing ideas which had been successful in the Rhodesian War. One of these was the 'Waxie' boot, as worn by this operator: made from soft calfskin with a neoprene wedge sole, it is a copy of the Rhodesian lightweight boot.

### E1: Recce Operator/Instructor, 1989
Recce training is full of challenges and pitfalls, some of the worst occurring during the capture and interrogation phase. During this phase of training the candidates are stripped naked, bound, and a hessian sack is tied over their heads for over four hours. Any hesitation or weakness shown by the candidates is exploited. Instructors are ruthless, since they know that should a candidate become an operator he could hold the lives of his team mates in his hands at critical moments.

During the selection and training phases instructors are allowed to wear uniforms that make them feel most comfortable. In this case the instructor wears a pair of Special Forces copy Portuguese camouflage shorts, a custom-made East German copy 'falling rain' camouflage smock, and a South-West Africa Special Forces camouflage cap with distinctive Germanic M43 style peak. The boots are Rhodesian lightweights, a prized possession in the Special Forces because of their soft leather. The chest webbing is Special Forces Pattern 80, holding three R-4/R-5 or AK-47/AKM 30-round magazines.

### E2: Major Wynand du Toit, 1987
In this compilation from photographs taken at the press conference shortly after his release from an Angolan prison, Major Du Toit wears the basic Permanent Force 'step-out' dress uniform with infantry branch, or 'Bokkop', collar badges. Above his left pocket are the ribbons for the (l. to r.) Pro Patria Medal, SADF 10 Year Service Medal, and the Chief of the SADF Commendation Medal; and the Free Fall Parachute Wing. Over the nameplate on the right breast are the first-class marksman's badge, or 'skietbalkie', and the numbered Recce Operator's Badge. The beret is standard SADF issue para type with the wire-embroidered Recce compass rose badge. The green, yellow, and black 'balkie' denotes that he has completed Recce training and is a qualified operator. A member of a support

African Special Forces (SWASPES) black nylon webbing vest; this was comfortable and durable, but despite the mesh shell was still hot, and never available in large quantities. He wears Rhodesian 'Clandestine' boots. His rifle is the Armscor R-5 5.56mm with a 50-round magazine and the Pattern 70 sling.

### D3: Recce Operator, 1984
A small Recce team, usually far behind enemy lines and unable to call upon conventional support, depended on maximum firepower for survival in the event of a contact. It was not uncommon for a four-man team to employ two

unit attached to the Recces would wear a different coloured bar according to parent corps. The shoulder flash worn on the right shoulder is for 4 Recce, based at Langebaan in Cape Province.

### E3: Colonel Jan Breytenbach, 1990

Commander of 1 Para Battalion, architect of the Recces, founder of 32 Battalion and the 44 Para Brigade Pathfinders, Colonel Jan Breytenbach, 'The Carpenter', is a legend in the SADF.

Above the left pocket of the *slangvel* he wears the free fall para instructor wings; over the right pocket are the 'skietbalkie' marksman badge, Recce Diver Badge, and Recce Operator Badge. The colonel's rank slip-ons are the embroidered 'bush pips'. Through his left shoulder strap he wears the instructor's lanyard which is simply a piece of woven nylon cord. The Reconnaissance Regiment stable

belt is worn with the compass rose belt buckle. The beret worn is standard Parabat type with a wire embroidered staff officer's badge. The SADF issue nutria trousers are tucked into jump boots.

### F1: OPS Medic, 7 Medical Battalion Group, 1990

Probably the least known of all SADF Special Forces units, 7 Medical Battalion Group personnel not only accompany most Recce teams but also 1 Para Battalion, 44 Para Brigade, the SAP Task Force, and the Chief of Staff Intelligence Units. (Not all 7 Med specialists are parachute-qualified.) This man wears a South African-manufactured Rhodesian camouflage Niemoller webbing vest which was specially made for the Chief of Staff Intelligence and 5 Recce but found its way to various other Special Forces units. His camouflage shirt and trousers are both Special Forces copies of Zimbabwean camouflage. (A pa-

*A South African Police Reaction Unit practising house clearing in Cape Town. Both men wear the second pattern camouflage uniform and carry folding-stock FN FALs. (South African Police)*

per label was sewn into each piece with 'Copy P', etc., the letters corresponding to each different pattern of camouflage that was copied.) He has a West German-manufactured helmet made of a Kevlar-type material layered between plastic. The cloth camouflage cover saw only limited use. His rifle bag and roll-up medical kit are both of Niemoller-type nylon. The boots are SADF jungle issue; both green and brown canvas versions existed.

## F2: South African Marine, 1988

South African Marines wore the standard issue SADF nutria uniform, earning them the nickname of the 'Brown Navy', which was taken as a mark of distinction by most Marines. The rank badges worn were similar to those worn by the Navy but rank titles differed (i.e., a Navy Able Seaman would be a Marine First Class). The badges were dark orange (rather than Navy yellow) printed on nutria cloth and were sewn onto brassards. Marines wore the standard Navy black beret with wire embroidered naval badges. Standard issue was the Pattern 70 webbing with the R-1 magazine pouches. The R-4, 5.56mm pouches were later provided, retaining the Pattern 70 designation. Stocks of the newer Pattern 83 equipment eventually filtered down to the Marines towards the end of their ten-year existence.

## F3: Navy Diver, 1989

Like most Special Forces the South African Navy divers put much emphasis on the 'buddy' system; when operating at extreme depths and sometimes in total darkness it is imperative to know your team mate and his limitations, as well as your own. Training is intense. Each day starts with a 12-kilometre run with weights. A simple uniform consisting of wetsuit trousers and a tightly woven sweater is often worn. Footwear is privately purchased running shoes, though beach runs can be made barefoot.

## G1: Constable, Koevoet, 1987

In the late years of Koevoet's existence negative SWAPO propaganda followed Koevoet's successes. As a direct result their commander, Col. Dreyer, ordered that all members wear the green bush uniform in place of the distinctive South-West African Police camouflage. Trousers, shorts, jackets, and both long and short sleeve shirts were made in both anti-infrared (AIR) and cotton blend materials. Clandestine boots became unobtainable, forcing Koevoet members to adopt different types of French or Israeli desert boots. Koevoet used the G-3 7.62mm rifle until replaced by the R-5 5.56mm rifle. Many Koevoet members preferred the AK/AKM family of weapons because of their durability and the ease of obtaining ammunition. Constables and officers were sometimes seen wearing the green 32 Battalion Cordura-type chest webbing.

## G2: Special Constable, Koevoet, 1985

This Special Constable wears the South-West African Police (SWAPOL) camouflage uniform, which was made in either standard cloth or an anti-infrared mesh cloth. Handguns were standard issue throughout the South African Police; Koevoet was issued with the Beretta Model 92S in 9mm Parabellum, the same handgun as issued to Johannesburg constables. The holster and belt worn are both Pattern 70 webbing. Black Koevoet members often preferred to wear a woollen balaclava which could be pulled down over the face on cold Kavango nights or rolled up to protect the head from the harsh sun during the day.

## G3: SAP Task Force (Koevoet), 1984

In its infancy some may have thought that Koevoet looked more like a rag-tag group of refugees than an élite unit. Equipment was not a matter of personal choice but of what was available. In this case the officer wears a field expedient chest webbing set stitched together from Pattern 70 kidney pouches. The belt is the SAP variant of the Pattern 70, with eyelets added to allow braces to be clipped directly to it. The water bottle is plastic, standard SADF Pattern 70. The boots are the Rhodesian model, though South Africa later made an almost exact copy of the Rhodesian 'Clandestine' boot.

## H1: Constable, South African Railway Police (SARP) Special Task Force, 1985

The Special Task Force adopted an SAS-type outlook to its training and activities and shrouded itself in secrecy. This constable wears the standard SARP camouflage shirt, trousers, and lightweight body armour with a camouflage cover. The ballistic fibre helmet with a built-in headphone and microphone allowed team members to communicate via a wireless transmitter/receiver. The weapons used varied and personal preference was allowed. This man carries a 9mm FN Browning Hi-Power pistol and a South African-manufactured stun grenade with a unique lock-over pin. The leather boots are standard SADF issue.

## H2: Staff Sergeant, South African Railway Police (SARP) Regional Task Force, 1985

The Railway Police Regional Task Force spent much of the latter period of their existence in black townships throughout South Africa, involved with unrest situations. This staff sergeant wears the standard SARP camouflage uniform. Sewn to the brassard on his left arm is the Regional Task Force yellow screen-printed shoulder flash and the two-piece rank badge. Above the right shirt pocket is a name tag and the screen-printed Regional Task Force wing. The SAP riot helmet was often seen worn with the visor removed. The belt is an SAP Pattern 70 variation, and the boots standard SADF issue. He carries the Stopper grenade launcher developed by Armscor specifically for riot situations; the Stopper fires a single 37mm tear gas, illumination, stun, or baton round.

## H3: Constable, South African Police Counter-Insurgency Unit, Rhodesia, 1969

The South African Police Counter-Insurgency Unit (SAPCOIN) gained a good measure of bush experience during their involvement in the Rhodesian War. This experience was later put to good use in South West Africa.

Both the SAP first and second pattern camouflage uniforms were manufactured in Rhodesia during the SAP's involvement there. This constable's Rhodesian-manufactured SAP second pattern flap-cap has the velcro fastening on the flap which distinguishes it from the South African-made version which used button snaps. Webbing equipment used by the COIN Units was supplied by the SAP, but constables occasionally substituted the Rhodesian-manufactured 7.62mm magazine pouches on their Pattern

61/64 webbing equipment. The Rhodesian camouflage jacket, as worn by this constable, held together in the thorny Rhodesian bush longer than the South African issue items. Weapons varied, but were in 7.62mm calibre; this constable carries the West German-manufactured G-3 with a 20-round magazine.

## I: Wings: South African Defence Force (SADF), South African Police (SAP), South African Railway Police (SARP)

(1) Sterling Silver Hunter Group mess dress parachute wing

(2) Embroidered Hunter Group parachute wing

(3) SAP Task Force gilded metal dress wing

*South African Police debussing from a Casspir armoured vehicle. The man kneeling on the right holding the FN MAG wears the second pattern camouflage uniform with cloth SAP emblem on the cap and brown name tape over the right breast pocket. (South African Police)*

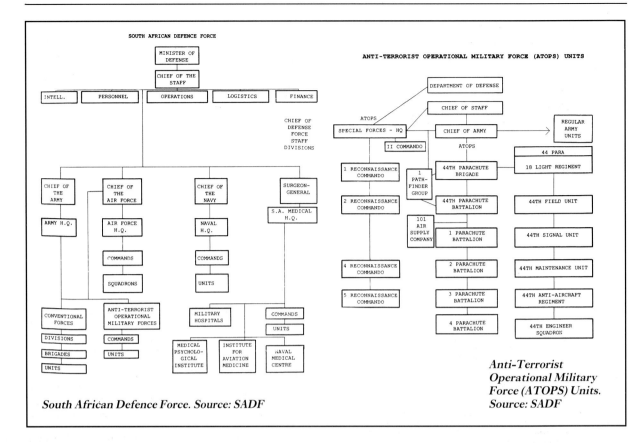

**South African Defence Force. Source: SADF**

*Anti-Terrorist Operational Military Force (ATOPS) Units. Source: SADF*

(4) SAP embroidered parachute wing (worn on camouflage uniform)

(5) SADF basic parachute dress wing

(6) SADF basic parachute instructor dress wing

(7) Junior Recce qualification wing, first type

(8) Junior Recce qualification wing, second type

(9) SARP Regional Task Force dress wing

(10) SARP Task Force gilded metal dress wing

(11) SARP Task Force embroidered parachute wing, first type

(12) SARP Task Force embroidered parachute wing, second type

*Background material* Upper half is SARP camouflage, and lower half is SAP first pattern camouflage.

## J: Insignia

(1) Hunter Group qualification shoulder flash. Three classes existed: silver scorpion on an infantry green background; red scorpion on a saffron background; and green scorpion on a saffron background. A dress version with the scorpion embroidered in fine gold wire on a black background also existed, though unofficially.

(2) 32 Battalion beret badge

(3) Reconnaissance Regiment wire embroidered beret badge

(4) South African Railway Police cap badge

(5) South African Police cap badge

(6) South African Corps of Marines breast badge

(7) 44 Parachute Brigade beret badge

(8) 3 Parachute Battalion beret badge (never officially approved, and soon withdrawn and replaced by 44 Para Brigade badge)

(9) 1 Parachute Battalion beret badge, first type

(10) 1 Parachute Battalion beret badge, second type or officer's version

*44 Parachute Battalion specialist pocket badges*:

(11) Pathfinder

(12) Anti-Tank Gunner

(13) Despatcher

*Background material* 32 Battalion camouflage: winter pattern (upper), and summer pattern (lower).

## K: Koevoet flashes

Each Koevoet group has its own distinctive shoulder insignia. Some units developed several variations over the years. The nine shoulder flashes shown here constitute the original South African Police units. Many of the words on the insignia are in the Owambo or Kavango dialect, the areas in South-West Africa where Koevoet operated.

(1) Ops K Rundu. Call sign Zulu 4 Kilo

(2) Nyime. Call sign Zulu 4 Juno

(3) Sizava. Call sign Zulu 4 November

(4) Mbindi. Call sign Zulu 4 Hotel

(5) Ruvadi. Call sign Zulu 4 Delta

(6) Nge. Call sign Zulu 4 Sierra

(7) Call sign Zulu 4 Whiskey

(8) Call sign Zulu 4 Echo. (Vier is number four in Afrikaans)

(9) Call sign Zulu 4 Foxtrot

*Background material* South African Police second pattern camouflage.

## L: Koevoet flashes

With the adoption of the green bush uniform the less active and more visible Koevoet units adopted the 'Tupperware' type shoulder flashes for use in public. As Koevoet expanded, new call signs were also created.

(1) South-West African Police Koevoet

(2) South-West African Police Counter Insurgency Unit

(3) South-West African Police Counter Insurgency Unit Kavango Area

(4) Zulu 8 Training Unit based at Oshakati

(5) Call sign Zulu 1 Hotel

(6) Call sign Zulu 1 Juno

*Background material* South-West African Police camouflage.

---

### Notes sur les planches en couleur

A1: On abandonne le casque d'acier en 1990, la blouse à quatre-poches, du style qui ressemble aux 'Denison' mais sans le rabat au niveau de l'entre-jambes; le fond et les genoux du pantalon sont renforcés; les bottes sont de fabrication anglaise; le parachute est un modèle T-10. A2: A noter le 'slangvel' caractéristique, le blouson actuel des parachutistes avec ses pièces grises de renforcement. Le casque israélien est de fabrication réglementaire d'Afrique du Sud. On le fabrique en vert et en marron mais il est d'habitude porté avec la toile 'nutria' par dessus avec la visière caractéristique. Equipement à motif 83, fusil R-4.5.56mm. A3: On ajoute une cravate couleur bordeaux, les guêtres blancs et l'insigne de la 44e Brigade pour les revues formelles. A noter que le parement de l'épaule et l'insigne de rang sont en tissu caoutchouté; les 'ailes' en métal du moniteur de parachute. La ceinture porte le mécanisme de la boucle singulière à la brigade; le béret de parachutiste porte l'insigne de la brigade et la barre en métal colorée pour désigner l'arme du service – ici c'est infanterie. A4: Les casques d'acier de fabrication anglaise 1941 sont parfois portés, en particulier par les officiers.

B1: Equipement à motif 70; sac à dos 'Para-Fox' vendu dans le commerce: la combinaison 'nutria' un choix personnel. B2: L'équipement à motif 61/64 a pour base le motif anglais 44, figuré ici en version plus ancienne – grand sac et de larges gibernes à munitions. L'uniforme de camouflage de premier motif de la 'Hunter Group' est acheté personnellement. B3: Uniforme de camouflage de second motif de la 'Hunter Group'; les variations d'hiver sont de couleur plus claire. Echarpe de voile rhodésienne, les bottes à boucles d'Afrique du Sud, équipement d'ordonnance 61/64, fusil R-1.

C1: L'équipement d'ordonnance avait da grands variations dans cette unité; à noter le gilet d'assaut rare en nylon à camouflage et le sac à dos. La tenue de camouflage d'été du bataillon, casquette à motif d'hiver; fusil R-4. C2: Equipement de poitrine en tissu de camouflage d'Afrique du Sud; ceinture d'équipement à motif 80. Uniforme de camouflage d'hiver du 32ème bataillon, casquette d'été, bottes 'clandestines' rhodésiennes. C3: Le kit et les habits sont assemblés par le particulier: le chapeau en tissu de camouflage à motif US MC ERDL; ancien motif de camouflage SADF, porté seulement par les unités de reconnaissance (Recce) après 1976; ceinture d'ordonnance à motif 80 avec l'étui à la hanche gauche. C4: Chemise 'nutria'; béret, insigne, cravate et ceinture de Police en tissu camouflage du 32ème bataillon.

D1: Tissu de camouflage noir et écru; équipement d'ordonnance à motif 80. Des copies d'uniformes de camouflage de l'Est sont fabriquées par l'Afrique du Sud et sont disponibles sur plusieurs motifs, ici un pantalon du Cuba, un T-shirt d'Allemagne de l'Est. D2: Copies d'une veste égyptienne, un pantalon portugais avec un gilet d'assaut des South West African Special Forces; fusil R-5. D3: Copies d'une veste de Libye, un pantalon français, casquette de brousse russe, bottes rhodésiennes; équipement local des Special Forces; mitraillette RPK.

E1: La copie d'un short portugais en tissu de camouflage et une blouse d'Allemagne de l'Est; la casquette des South West African Special Forces; les bottes rhodésiennes; équipement de poitrine à motif 80. E2: Tenue de la Permanent Force avec insigne d'infanterie au col, béret de parachutiste avec l'insigne de l'unité de Recce; à la poitrine gauche on voit les rubans de la Pro Patria pour les dix années de service, les médailles pour être chef du SADF, les ailes du parachute de tombée-libre; sur le coté droit on voit les insignes de qualification du tireur d'élite de première classe et de Recce; à l'épaule droite le parement du 4ème régiment Recce. E3: Le 'père' du SASF porte le 'slangvel' de parachutiste avec les ailes du moniteur de tombée-libre; à droite les insignes de tireur d'élite, plongeur de Recce; à l'épaule gauche se trouve le cordon simple du moniteur. Ceinture du régiment de Recce; béret de parachutiste avec insigne de l'officier d'état major.

F1: Les gilets d'équipement d'ordonnance de type rhodésiens 'Niemoller' sont rares et fabriqués sur les lieux; copies locales de l'uniforme de camouflage du Zimbabwe;

### Farbtafeln

A1: Stahlhelme wurden 1990 auslaufen gelassen; lose Bluse mit 4 Taschen ähnlich wie "Denison", aber ohne Leistenklappe; Hose mit verstärktem Sitz und Knien; britische Stiefel, Fallschirm Modell T-10. A2: Siehe typische "Slangvel", die gegenwärtige Fallschirmjäger-Jacke mit grauen Verstärkungsflecken. Der israelische Helm wird unter Lizenz in Südafrika in Grün wie in Braun hergestellt, meist aber mit einer Nutria-Stoffbespannung mit charakteristischem Sonnenschirm. Gurten Muster 83, 5,56mm-Gewehr R-4. A3: Für Paradezwecke kamen ein braunes Halstuch mit 44 Bde.-Abzeichen und weiße Gamaschen hinzu. Siehe 44 Bde.-Schulteraufschlag und Rangabzeichen aus Gummistoff, Freifall-Metallschwingen für Fallschirmjäger-Instruktor, Gürtel mit Brigadeschnalle, Fallschirmjäger-Kappe mit Brigadeabzeichen und farbiger Metallstreifen für Waffengattung – hier Infanterie. A4: Britische Stahlhelme von 1941 wurden gelegentlich getragen, besonders von Offizieren.

B1: Gurten, Muster 70; kommerzieller Para-Fox-Rucksack, einteiliger Nutria-Overall mit persönlicher Wahl. B2: Gurten, Muster 61/64, beruhend auf britischem Muster 44, in früherer Version mit großem Ranzen und breiten Munitionstaschen. Hunter Group-Tarnuniform des ersten Musters, privat erworben; Gewehr R-1. B3: Zweites Muster der Hunter Group-Tarnuniform; Winterversionen hatten hellere Farben. Rhodesisches Netzhalstuch, frühe südafrikanische Schnallenstiefel, Gurten 61/64, Gewehr R-1.

C1: Gurtenausrüstung variierte stark in dieser Einheit; siehe seltene Nylon-Tarnweste DPM und Rucksack. Sommer-Tarnuniform des 32. Bataillons, Winterkappe, Gewehr R-4. C2: Südafrikanische Brustgurtenausrüstung in Tarnfarbe; Gürtelausrüstung Muster 80. Winter-Tarnuniform des 32. Bataillons, Sommerkappe; rhodesische "Anschleich"-Stiefel. C3: Persönlich zusammengestellte Kleidung und Ausrüstung: Tarnhut USMC ERDL, Tarnuniform nach frühem SADF-Muster, nur von Erkundungseinheiten nach 1976 getragen; Gürtel Muster 80 mit "Flucht- und Schleich"-Tasche an linker Hüfte. C4: Nutria-Hmd, spezielle Tarn-Polizeikappe, Rangabzeichen, Halstuch und Gürtel.

D1: Schwarze Tarncreme, spurenlose Stiefel, Gurtenausrüstung Muster 80; südafrikanische Kopien von Tarnuniformen der Otblock-Staaten waren in vielen Mustern erhältlich – hier kubanische Hose, ostdeutsches T-shirt. D2: Kopien von ägyptischer Jacke, portugiesischer Hose, schwarze Nylonweste der Südwestafrikanischen Special Forces, Gewehr R-5. D3: Kopien der libyschen Jacke und französischen Hose, russischer Buschhut, rhodesische Stiefel, Gurte der Special Forces, Maschinengewehr RPK.

E1: Kopiert nach portugiesischen Tarn-Shorts und ostdeutscher Bluse; Kappe der Südwestafrikanischen Special Forces, rhodesische Stiefel, Brustgurtenausrüstung Muster 80. E2: Ausgeh-Uniform der regulären Truppen mit Infanterie-Kragenabzeichen, Kappe der Fallschirmjäger mit Aufklärungsabzeichen, auf linker Brustseite Abzeichen von Pro Patria, 10 Jahre Dienst, Auszeichnungsmedaillen der SADF, und Freifall-Fallschirmjägerschwingen; rechts, Brust Scharfschützenabzeichen und Recce-Qualifikationsabzeichen; auf rechter Schulter Abzeichen des 4. Aufklärungs-regiments. E3: Der "Vater" der Südwestafrikanischen Special Forces trägt Para-Slangvel mit Freifall-Instruktor-Schwingen; rechts, Scharfschütze, Recce-Taucher, Recce-Abzeichen; einfache Instruktorschnur auf linker Schulter. Gürtel des Recce-Regiments; Para-Kappe mit Stabsoffiziers-Abzeichen.

F1: Seltene, lokal angefertigte rhodesische Tarnweste vom Typ "Niemoller"; lokale Kopien der simbawischen Tarnuniform; Helm aus Westdeutschland. F2: Standard-SADF-Nutria-Uniform, mit marineartigen Abzeichen, aber in Dunkelorange; Marine-infanteristen trugen schwarze Marinekappen und Marine-Abzeichen. Gurten Muster 70, Gewehr R-1. F3: Kleidung für Morgenlauf, Schwimmanzug-Hose und enger Pullover.

G1: Späte Koevoet-Uniform, durchwegs grün, um sie von Einheiten in casque d'Allemagne de l'Ouest. **F2:** Uniforme réglementaire de SADF 'nutria' avec l'insigne de style marin mais orange-foncé; les Marines portent les bérets noirs de la Navy et les insignes de la Navy. Equipement à motif 70, fusil R-1. **F3:** Tenue pour la course matinale: pantalon de la combinaison de plongée et un pullover serré.

**G1:** L'uniforme 'Koevoet' est vert uni pour qu'on puisse le distinguer des unités camouflées qu'on accuse des atrocités; on porte parfois l'équipement d'ordonnance de 32ème Bataillon; les fusils sont un mélange de types G-3, R-5 et AK. **G2:** Uniforme de camouflage SWAPOL, passe-montagne populaire en laine; pistolet d'ordonnance automatique Beretta. **G3:** Cette tenue est fabriquée de tout ce qui est disponible; équipement de poitrine fabriquée sur les lieux avec les étuis à motif 70.

**H1:** Tenue de camouflage SARP et armure renforcée; casque avec le matériel de radio; Pistolet Browning automatique et grenade 'Stun' sud africaine. **H2:** Uniforme de camouflage SAFP avec le parement à l'épaule de la Regional Task Force; casque de police anti-émeutes; lanceur de grenade 'Stopper'. **H3:** Casquette rhodésienne de deuxième motif. Veste de camouflage rhodésienne; le mélange entre les équipements 61/64 et celui de Rhodésie est commun; fusil G-3.

**I:** Pour les identifications des insignes de qualification 'wings', voir la liste dans les légende I1 à I12 en anglais. A l'arrière plan on voit le camouflage de la South Africa Railway Police (en haut), le camouflage à premier motif de la South Africa Police (en bas).

**J:** Pour identifier ces insignes voir les légendes en anglais J1 à J13. A l'arrière plan on voit le camouflage d'hiver du 32ème bataillon (en haut), puis les motifs pour l'été (en bas).

**K:** Les insignes du 'Koevoet' (South West African Police Counter-Insurgency) sont fabriqués à l'intérieur de l'unité et portés commeparements et motifs sur les T-shirts. Les indicatifs d'appel de radio comme 'Zulu 4 Kilo' identifient les groupes de combat avec trente hommes et quatre véhicules. Voir les légendes en anglais pour les identifications. Arrière plan: camouflage de 2ème motif de la SAP.

**L:** Insigne 'Koevoet' plus ancien, fabriqué en parement d'étoffe caoutchouté (Tupperware), porté en public sur l'uniforme vert uni plus ancien. Voir les légendes en anglais. Arrière plan: camouflage de la South West African Police.

Tarnuniformen zu unterscheiden, denen Grausamkeiten vorgeworfen wurden; 32 Bn. grüne Brustgurten-Ausrüstung wurde gelegentlich getragen; die Gewehre waren gemischt: G-3, R-5 und AK-Modelle. **G2:** SWAPOL-Tarnuniform, mit beliebter Woll-Balaclava und automatischer Beretta-Pistole. **G3:** Kleidung und Ausrüstung zusamengewürfelt aus allem, was verfügbar war: lokal hergestellte Brustgurten aus Taschen, Muster 70.

**H1:** SARP-Tarnuniform mit kugelsicherem Überwurf, Helm mit Funkanlage, Browning Automatikpistole, südafrikanische Stun-Granate. **H2:** SARP-Tarniform mit Schulterabzeichen der Regional Task Force, Polizeihelm, Stopper-Granatwerfer. **H3:** Rhodesische SAP-Kappe, rhodesische Tarnjacke; gemischte Gurten 61/64 und rhodesischer Art waren weit verbreitet, Gewehr G-3.

**I:** Qualifikations-Schwingen – siehe Identifikationsliste in englischen Bildtexten I1–I12. Hintergrund (oben): Südafrikanische Eisenbahnpolizei-Tarnuniform, (unten): Südafrikanische Polizei-Tarnuniform, erstes Muster.

**J:** Insignien – siehe englische Bildtexte J1–J13 für Indentifizierung. Hintergrund (oben): 32 Bn. Winter-Tarnuniform, (unten): Sommeruniformen.

**K:** "Koevoet"-(südwestafrikanische Anti-Rebellen-Einheit) Insignien, innerhalb der Einheiten angefertigt und als Abyeichen und T-Shirt-Motive getragen. Die Funkruf-Erkennungssignale wie z.B. "Zulu 4 Kilo" identifizierten 30-köpfige Kampfgruppen in vier Fahrzeugen. Siehe englische Bildtexte für Identifizierungen. Hintergrund: SAP-Tarnuniform 2. Muster.

**L:** Späte "Koevoet"-Abzeichen aus Gummistoff (Tupperware), öffentlich getragen auf den späteren grünen Uniformen. Siehe englische Bildtexte. Hintergrund: Südwestafrikanische Polizei-Tarnuniform.